The Purposive Self and the Dreaming Mind

To order additional copies, please contact us.
BookSurge
www.booksurge.com
1-866-308-6235
orders@booksurge.com

The Purposive Self and the Dreaming Mind

Frank Faranda

2009

For Heidi and Oliver

Table of Contents

Chapter One: Introduction

In recent years, theories of the self have increasingly come to occupy a prime position in many schools of psychological theory and dynamic psychotherapy. These theories include ideas of self development (Stern, 1985), self representation (Jacobson, 1964), self regulation (Emde, 1983), true self (Winnicott, 1968), Self Psychology (Kohut, 1971, 1977), and multiplicity of self (Bromberg, 1993, 1996). Sutherland (1993) discusses one of the primary aspects of the theoretical convergence on this construct. He states

> Several trends have contributed to the recent emergence of the self as a central issue within psychoanalysis. Common to all these trends is a growing awareness that the fundamental assumptions of psychoanalysis did not do justice to new clinical findings...more recent theories have increasingly seen pathological manifestations as being involved with the person as a whole, that is, the self. (p.3)

This convergence offers both opportunity and challenge. The opportunity stems from the potential for shared insight and mutual scientific advancement; the challenge stems from the varied use of the term and the imprecision of definition. As a construct, the self is ripe for misunderstanding and by its very colloquial nature it eludes understanding.

In studying the varied usage of the term *self*, there emerges one area of self-experience that has been relatively undeveloped: the self as a purposive function distinct from the functions of the ego. This aspect of the theory of the self is observable in nascent form beginning with the work of Freud, extending through Ego Psychology, Object Relations, and Self Psychology. That it is simultaneously pervasive and absent is one of its paradoxical qualities; in attempting to locate it, it is elusive and enigmatic. And without an adequate system of description for this particular aspect of the self, it is difficult to name and difficult to discuss. In this essay, it will be referred to as the Purposive Self: a series of functional processes within the psyche that move the personality toward integration, psychological healing, and ongoing development.

Frank Faranda

The traditions of dream interpretation within psychodynamic treatment begin with Freud in 1900. In his epochal work, <u>The Interpretation of Dreams,</u> Freud forged an entire system of psychology based on the notion that the dream is a deception aimed at maintaining equilibrium. But this was not the only theory being developed. Jung was developing his own ideas based on his experience with the symbolic material of schizophrenics. Jung found that the psyches of these individuals were producing meaningful communications aimed, he believed, at achieving integration and furthering healing. Jung applied these ideas to the symbolic experience of dreaming and discovered similar patterns of purpose and intention. Like Freud, Jung built a model of the mind that was capable of accounting for the dream. For Freud, the mind was founded on repression, deception, and the maintenance of pleasure; for Jung, the mind was creative, intentional, and spiritually anchored.

The Self and the Dream will be explored as they intersect along the axis of Purpose. Toward this end, psychoanalytic theory of the self will be reviewed to bring into relief the purposive processes in relation to other aspects of the self. Psychoanalytic dream theory will be studied, beginning with Freud's model, and continuing to the present in order to uncover the patterns of change in the use of dreams that reveal areas of deficit in the underlying dream theory. Following these explorations, this essay will examine Jungian ideas on the Self and the Dream. Embedded in the Jungian model of the mind is an understanding of the self as an intentional center of the personality. Manifestations of the Purposive Self in the Jungian model appear in the function of the dream, transference phenomena, and in all psychoanalytic derivatives. According to Jung, the Self has a healing potential that animates what Jungians refer to as the process of individuation: a process whereby a person becomes him- or herself through the ongoing differentiation and development of self in relation to challenges in the environment.

The final goal of this essay will be to facilitate a dialogue between psychoanalytic and the Jungian perspectives. Through a detailed case study, a model of treatment based on an integration of psychoanalytic and Jungian ideas will be outlined and discussed. It is hoped that through this discussion, the possibility of developing additional, more comprehensive, models of treatment will become possible.

Chapter Two: The Self in Psychoanalytic Theory:
Person, Core, and Process

Introduction: The Ubiquitous and Ill-defined Self

The construct of the self in psychoanalytic theory is both ubiquitous and ill defined (Lesser, 1978; Tuttman, 1988). Beginning with Freud's irregular usage of *das ich*, confusion has surrounded this concept and uncertainty about the domain of inquiry and the nature of what was being defined have plagued theorists (Rangell, 1980; Levin, 1969). Yet even with this tentative history, the construct of the self has steadily grown in importance until today where it occupies a prominent position in most schools of psychoanalytic theory (Friedland, 1978; Sutherland, 1993; Gedo & Goldberg, 1973; Lachmann, 1996). Related disciplines, such as neurobiology and infant research, have also increasingly come to use the self as an anchoring concept (Schore, 1994; Gedo, 1999a). These three phenomena—the uncertainty of definition, the steady progress toward a ubiquitous usage, and the cross discipline convergence on this construct—present the current day psychodynamic clinician with both an opportunity and a burden. The opportunity lies in the potential for increased ability to communicate with a common language as well as the possibility of cross-discipline validation. The burden stems from the fact that even with these emerging potentials, it is nearly impossible to know precisely what anyone means when they say 'the self'.

This chapter will attempt to address this paradox through achieving a clearer understanding of three interrelated areas: 1) what are the different aspects of the human experience that are being defined as the self; 2) what is the historical arc leading to the present day conceptualizations; and 3) what influences, both within psychoanalysis and within the general culture, have contributed to this evolution. Finally, through this survey, it is hoped that a clearer vision of the Purposive Self will come into relief.

Frank Faranda

Three Domains of Self

The self has been defined variously as: an internal object representation (Sandler & Rosenblatt, 1962); the regulatory system of the personality (Gedo & Goldberg, 1973); an autonomous variable independent of the instincts (Hartmann, 1939); something that is only observable through interpersonal relations (Sullivan, 1940); that which is found inside the boundaries of the skin (Winnicott, 1949); the supra-ordinate functions of the personality (Hartmann, 1950); that which maintains continuity of the personality over time and space (Kohut, 1977; Lachmann, 1996); the part of the personality that develops in relationship (Winnicott, 1962); the whole person (Freud, 1915; Kohut, 1977); that which seeks individuation (Mahler et al., 1975); a primary identity (Lichtenstein, 1977); a non-communicative aspect of the personality (Winnicott, 1963); an illusion (Sullivan, 1940); that which follows innate tendencies toward the development of cohesion in the personality (Kohut, 1977; Lichtenstein, 1977); a series of relationally governed, decentered, discontinuous states (Bromberg, 1993, 1996); that which is true and authentic in a person (Winnicott, 1960); and a system of affective regulatory functions internalized in infancy that constitute the core of the person (Emde, 1983).

The above list is neither definitive nor exhaustive. Rather, it represents what has come to be a very confusing terrain. In the simplest of terms, the self means many different things to many different people. Lesser (1978) states that when she looked up 'self' in the card catalog at NYU Medical School she found that

> The theory of self in contemporary psychoanalysis includes the following items for cross-references: body, human; consciousness; ego; identity; individuality; mind and body; personality; role-playing; super ego; thought and thinking; will. A long list—one that encompasses most of psychology. Although I have not researched all of these topics, I have found that concepts of self are both complex and obscure. (p. 545)

And although, Tuttman (1988) is correct when he states that the "tension between alternate theories makes for productive contemplation and stimulates advance in the field" (p. 216), it appears that some attempt at contextualization, leading to a functional categorization, might be warranted in order to facilitate a more fruitful contemplation and a more usable clinical theory of the self.

In considering the multitude of definitions of the self it becomes clear that the differences in definition are not merely a function of theoretical orientation, nor are they completely explainable as the product of a general increase in objectivity. Rather, it appears as if, in addition to these two potential hypotheses, the reason for the variability in definition is due to other factors. This essay puts forth the thesis that the multitude of existing formulations for the construct of the self, does not only reflect the theoretical imperatives of any particular theory or theorist, nor does it merely indicate an inability to accurately perceive, but rather, it reflects the fact that the object of study, the self, is not simply one entity, but instead, three, each distinct and with its own formulaic context. These three areas refer to the whole of the person, the core of the person, and the functioning of the person. In the language of this essay, these three areas will be termed the *Self as Person*, the *Self as Core*, and the *Self as Process,* respectively. Before proceeding to define these three areas of the self, it needs to be noted that this taxonomy of the self is hypothetical in that these three areas exist in a concentricity of human meaning that often defies discrete analysis.

The *Self as Person* refers both to the subjective and the objective experience of the whole person. This forms the center of all psychoanalytic self-concepts and in many ways constitutes a comprehensive umbrella for all theories of the self. In this are ideas related to unity (Wolstein, 1975; Lachmann, 1996), self-representation (Sandler & Rosenblatt, (1962) and identity (Erickson, 1963). The *Self as Core* refers to ideas that conceive of something at the center of a person. In this aspect of self theory are concepts such as ground plan (Lichtenstein, 1977), True Self (Winnicott, 1949, 1962), or affective core (Emde, 1983). The *Self as Process* refers to any number of functions that are attributed to the self or related to the maintenance of the self. These include conceptions such as the autonomous functions of the ego (Hartmann, 1939, 1950), the maturational processes of the self (Winnicott, 1960, 1962), the cohesive tendencies of the self (Kohut, 1977), the supraordinate self (Saperstein & Gaines, 1973), the fourth metapsychological function (Lichtenstein, 1977), as well as, the relational processes of dyadic affect regulation and attunement in infancy (Emde, 1983; Stern, 1985; Tronick, 1989).

5

In the following section, an historical review of the theory of the self will be offered with an eye toward uncovering the relationship of psychoanalytic theory to the notion of a Purposive Self. This review will begin with Freud and follow through Ego Psychology, Object Relations, Self Psychology, contemporary relational models, and infant developmental theory.

Historical Changes in the Three Domains of Self
  Freud

The confusion over the nature and scope of the self within psychoanalytic theory began with Freud's choice of *das ich* to refer to the psychological person (Rangell, 1980; Ticho, 1980). This concept of the psychological person became entangled with the concept of the ego as it developed with the structural model after 1923 (Hartmann, 1956; Tuttman, 1988). Ticho (1980) suggests that there are two different uses of *das ich* in Freud's writings, one prior to 1923 and one after. As Ticho, (1980) states

> It seems possible to detect two main uses of Ich: one in which the term distinguishes a person's self as a whole (including perhaps, his body) from other people, and the other in which it denotes a particular part of the mind characterized by special attributes and functions. (p. 850)

Compounding this lack of distinction was Strachey's uniform translation of *das ich* to ego (McIntosh, 1986). Lost with this translation was the distinction between the *Self as Person* and the ego as a structural sphere where conflict becomes resolved (Tuttman, 1988). Hartmann (1956) was the first to suggest that Freud's pre-structural use of *das ich* be understood as referring to the self. This pre-structural use is most evident in Freud's (1915) <u>On Narcissism</u> where the notion of a narcissistic cathexis of the person first became postulated (Tuttman, 1988; Gedo, & Goldberg, 1973). This linking of the self to the question of narcissism remained unfinished by Freud (Hartmann, 1950, 1958; Kohut, 1971, 1977). Contextualizing this phenomenon, Gedo and Goldberg, (1973) state that the question of narcissism and the self embedded within this context was not as important to Freud as was the ego and that it remained for future generations to complete his early speculations.

Heinz Hartmann

Heinz Hartmann (1939, 1948, 1950, 1956) struggled to give shape to certain facets of the human experience he perceived as inadequately developed in Freud's work (Lichtenstein, 1977; Sutherland, 1993). Lichtenstein (1977) believes that Hartmann was attempting to understand the evolutionary development of the structures of the mind Freud had proposed. For Hartmann, Freud's pleasure principle was insufficient to account for the development of the ego. Specifically, Hartmann found it impossible to explain the origination of the ego as a mental structure by considering only the drives of sex and aggression and their impact with reality (Lichtenstein, 1977). As a supplement, Hartmann (1939) begins an elaboration of the concept of the ego to include the autonomous functions of synthesis and adaptation. In later papers, Hartmann (1948, 1950, 1956) expands this effort by suggesting that this area of the personality be redefined as "the self."

Within Hartmann's work furthering ego psychology, are the seeds for a number of important advancements in the understanding of the self. Hartmann's work can be seen to expand, principally, the domains of the *Self as Core* and the *Self as Process*. The specific contributions that have influenced or advanced our conceptualization of the self in these areas include, a proposed independent line of development for the "autonomous organizing functions;" a "conflict-free sphere" of the person; speculations on functions of self-regulation as independent of the ego; narcissism as independent of sexual libido; and speculations of the question of inherited potentials.

Hartmann begins this work in 1939 when he proposes an expansion of Ego Psychology to include a "conflict free sphere of the ego" where the autonomous ego functions of synthesis and adaptation are in operation. He states (1939)

> The full range of synthetic factors is not yet known: some of them belong to the superego, most of them to the ego, and some of these belong partly to the conflict-free regulative functions of the ego. (p. 75)

As is clear from Hartmann's choice of words, these early speculations include the caveat that much remains unknown. Also clear is the notion that for Hartmann, the "organizing function of the ego," performs what he believes is a self-regulatory act. Following the three-domain model of the self proposed in this essay, Hartmann's work on synthesis and adaptation translates into functions of self-regulation and self-preservation that fall under the rubric of the *Self as Process.*

By 1948 Hartmann was expanding his work on the self, exploring the links of the self-preservative functions to several key ideas within the general theory of Ego Psychology. The first element that concerned Hartmann was the differentiation of the energies of self-preservation from the energies of libido. Although Hartmann (1948) is reluctant to postulate a separate "drive" for self-regulation, he states that these energies constitute a "third force" (in addition to the instincts and reality) and are not merely desexualized libido (Lichtenstein, 1977). This emendation in the understanding of drives constituted a significant gain in the differentiation of the self from the ego. Hartmann (1948), however, states that his conceptions were simply following an already existent, albeit undeveloped, area of Freud's work: the ego drives. He states, "Actually, in the course of the development of psychoanalytic theory, they [the ego drives] gradually, more or less, lost their status as an independent unit" (p. 382). And in support of this, he quotes Freud (1940) as saying, "the ego sets itself the task of self-preservation which the id seems to reject" (In Hartmann, 1948, p. 383). What Hartmann left unstated in 1948 was that, unlike Freud, he was beginning to postulate an independent energy source that guided self-regulation and that had a separate line of development. Regarding this he states (1948)

> Self regulation can be defined on different levels...there is one level of self-regulation which corresponds to what we usually call synthetic functions of the ego or, as I prefer to call it, an organizing function: it balances the psychic systems against each other and regulates the relationship between the individual and his environment. (p. 384)

In this, Hartmann is not only postulating an expansion of the concept of the ego and the inclusion of self-regulation, but he is stipulating that the self-regulatory function of the self operates in relation to the environment. This shift toward the use of a relational model as a means of understanding the functioning of the self continued to develop within psychoanalytic theory leading up to the present contemporary models of the self.

Additional efforts by Hartmann in 1950 and 1956, included the exploration of narcissism as it relates to self-preservation and the "whole person," increased clarification of the autonomous functions, and, the most trouble-some concept he approached, the question of inherited potentials.

In speaking of a narcissistic cathexis, Hartmann (1950) makes the following distinction between the ego and the self

> a differentiation of these concepts [self and ego] appears essential...the one refers to the self (one's own person) in contradistinction to the object, the second to the ego (as a psychic system) in contradistinction to the other substructures of the personality...it therefore will be clarifying if we define narcissism as the libidinal cathexis not of the ego but of the self. (pp. 84-85)

Clearly, at this stage in Hartmann's work he was separating the *Self as Person* from the ego functions (Lesser, 1978) and the study of narcissism was the avenue he was taking to arrive at this distinction. Implicit in this idea was a departure from the Ego Psychological conception of libido as sexual and the formulation that any other energy observed was to be understood as desexualized or sublimated. Hartmann laid the groundwork for a model of psychic energy capable of supporting an understanding of the autonomous self-regulatory functions of the *Self as Process*. Hartmann, however, never formally challenged Freud's metapsychology with a revision of the theory of psychic energy. He states (1950)

> The question whether all energy at the disposal of the ego originates in the instinctual drives, I am not prepared to answer. Freud thinks that 'nearly all of the energy' active in the psychic apparatus comes from the drives, thus pointing to the possibility that part of it may have a different origin. But what other sources of mental energy may there be?...it may be that some of it originates in what I describe as the autonomous ego. (pp. 86-87)

Hartmann's tentativeness in questioning Freud's theory of psychic energy necessitated an equally tentative formulation for the autonomy of the *Self as Process*.

Thus far, the focus has been on Hartmann's theoretical innovations of the *Self as Person,* with his reassignment of narcissistic cathexis to the self, and the *Self as Process* with his reformulation of the synthetic and self-regulatory

Frank Faranda

functions. The final element in Hartmann's work that remains to be illuminated relates to the *Self as Core*. In 1950 Hartmann began to develop the idea that the developmental potentials of the person were in existence prior to relational influence. In support of this, Hartmann (1950) quotes Freud (1937) as saying

> We have no reason to dispute the existence and importance of primal, congenital ego-variations...when we speak of 'archaic inheritance' we are generally thinking only of the id and apparently we assume that an ego was not existent at the beginning of the individual's life. But we must not overlook the fact that id and ego are originally one, and it does not imply a mystical overestimation of heredity if we think it credible that, even before the ego exists, its subsequent lines of development, tendencies and reactions are already determined. (Freud, 1937; in Hartmann, 1950, p. 79)

From this Hartmann found support for the idea that the self had a separate line of development independent of the ego, the id, and the sexual/aggressive drives. These speculations into what exists within the infant at birth, in addition to the id, reflected Hartmann's nascent explorations into what has been elaborated in recent years in the fields of infant research (Stern, 1985; Emde, 1983) and infant neurobiology (Schore, 1994). But beyond Hartmann's proposed developmental revisions was the deeper question of whether there exists an innate and unique predisposition for the personality; what might be referred to as an apriori biological inheritance for personality. This would refer to what Lichtenstein (1977) states as "the awareness that survival in man must refer to survival as a unique person, an individual capable of living a life in possession of his 'true self' [Winnicott,1952]" (p.237). But Lichtenstein also states somewhat equivocally that

> Hartmann's derivation of primary ego autonomy from inherited biological propensities has been subject to criticism. I myself have expressed certain conceptual reservations about the entelechetic and aprioistic implications of such concepts. (p. 226)

What makes these conceptualizations of the *Self as Core* difficult for psychoanalysis, as Lichtenstein and Freud both intimate, is their proximity to unver-

10

ifiable metaphysical notions such as spirit and soul. Also important, although unacknowledged at that point in psychoanalytic history, is their proximity to Freud's metapsychology and the implicit revisions in that metapsychology that would be required to account for these new ideas.

When taken together, Hartmann's innovations on the construct of the self provide all the necessary elements for conceptualizing a model of the Purposive Self: innate developmental plan as biological propensity; independent source of psychic energy separate from the drives and the ego; and a basic tendency toward self-regulation. That these advancements have remained somewhat unacknowledged is due to two factors: one, Hartmann's political position within Ego Psychology; and two, the lack of an adequate epistemology for appreciating and contextualizing his contributions.

Hartmann was committed both to the maintenance of Freud's legacy in the form of Ego Psychology (Tuttman, 1988) and to the advancement of psychoanalytic thinking (Lichtenstein, 1977). These two allegiances constituted a tension that rendered Hartmann both creatively inspired and politically bound. In other words, he attempted to expand psychoanalytic understanding of the self as a construct without abandoning Freud's metapsychology or the structural theory. This conflict for Hartmann related to the broader question of whether a scientific epistemology, such as the one envisioned by Jones and Strachey, was essentially at odds with the idea of a Purposive Self which tends to be linked to the epistemologies of religion and literature (Newirth, 2001). And it is further proposed that this inability of psychoanalytic theory to navigate between what might be considered *epistemological self-states,* exerts a continual marginalizing pressure upon any theory that illuminates the question of purpose as a function of the self.

D. W. Winnicott

Days before his death, Winnicott responded to a letter from a French translator of his work (reported in Schacht, 1988). The letter was written to Winnicott to get clarification on the meaning of the term *self* as used by him in his paper, <u>On the Basis of the Self in the Body</u>, (1970). Winnicott wrote back stating that he had a great deal of uncertainty about what constituted the self. After a lifetime of work elucidating this area of human experience, doing as much to help psychoanalysis understand the self as any other single

11

theorist (Greenberg & Mitchell, 1983), and on the eve of his death, he still had to acknowledge that the meaning of the term remained elusive.

In the present brief survey of Winnicott's ideas on the self, several themes will become illuminated: 1.) Winnicott's model of the self relies heavily on relational dynamics in its formulation; 2.) Winnicott's ideas on the self extend into all three domains of *Person, Core,* and *Process*; 3.) Winnicott stops short of fully elaborating the theoretical principles for a Purposive Self that were implicit in his speculations into the working of the mind.

The Self as Person

Winnicott (in Schacht, 1988) begins to formulate his ideas on the meaning of the self by comparing it to the concept of the ego. He states

> I think that the user of the term self is on a different platform from the user of the word ego. The first platform has to do with life and living in a direct way; the second, here the word le moi is used, the speaker or writer is more detached, less involved, perhaps clearer because of being able to use all that there is of the intellectual approach. (p. 516)

For Winnicott then, an understanding of the self begins with the experience of being. Also of note in this formulation is the implicit ineffability of the self: The self is both something we all know subjectively through experience and simultaneously, something we are at a loss to name.

Much earlier, Winnicott (1962) speaks of the developmental differences between the self and the ego. He states

> The term ego can be used to describe that part of the growing human personality that tends, under suitable conditions, to become integrated into a unit...It will be seen that the ego offers itself for study long before the word self has relevance. The word self arrives after the child has begun to use intellect to look at what others see or feel or hear and what they conceive when they meet this infant body.... (p. 56)

Winnicott reveals in this statement the ways in which his work grew out of the context of the structural model. According to that schema, the ego is a unit system that becomes integrated over time and is involved in conflict with other structures of the personality. What Winnicott begins to postulate, is that, unlike the ego, the self emerges, not through intrapsychic conflict, but through relationship and intersubjectivity. For Winnicott this parallels the work of Klein on the attainment of the depressive position.

A related aspect of the *Self as Person* that Winnicott elaborates is the link of the self to the body and to the skin as boundary of the self. This is the "self that is but newly established is a unit with a 'skin'" (Winnicott, 1963a, p. 99). Boundaries, for Winnicott, constitute one of the primary elements of the self; and the body is the first means the infant uses in delineating self from other. The self is what forms when the infant begins to establish the me and the not-me (Schacht, 1988). For Winnicott, there is no such thing as an infant, in that the self of the infant exists only in the context of a relationship with the self of the mother and only through ongoing development does a shell of the self begin to form.

As early as 1948 Winnicott writes, "The mental health of the human being is laid down in infancy by the mother, who provides an environment in which complex but essential processes in the infant's self can become completed" (p xx). He also states, "The self essentially recognizes itself in the eyes and facial expression of the mother and in the mirror which can come to represent the mother's face" (in Schacht 1988, p.516). For Winnicott, a failure of the mother to adapt to the infant results in an annihilation of the self (Winnicott, 1962, 1963). In these formulations, Winnicott expresses what might be understood as his most central contribution to understanding infant development, and by implication, an understanding of the self: the importance of the relationship with the mother (Bacal, 1990). His emphasis on the relational component constitutes a dramatic shift from the work of Freud and Klein and parallels the shift away from the construct of the ego and toward the construct of the self. As Winnicott states, (in Schacht, 1988), "The self awakes in the mutuality of the relationship" (p. 526).

The Self as Core

Moving beyond Winnicott's ideas on the *Self as Person,* one encounters several areas in his work where paradox makes understanding more difficult. The clearest example of this paradox is to be found in Winnicott's formulation for the *Self as Core,* the True Self. Central to his formulations on the origin and development of the True Self is the idea that the innermost core is linked to the body's basic sense of being alive. He states (1960a)

> The True Self appears as soon as there is any mental organization of the individual at all, and it means little more than the summation of sensori-motor aliveness. (p. 149)

And from the same source

> The True Self comes from the aliveness of the body tissues and the working of body-functions, including the heart's action and breathing. It is closely linked with the idea of Primary Process, and is, at the beginning, essentially not reactive to external stimuli, but primary. (p. 148)

Thus, to begin, Winnicott appears to liken the True Self to the basic sense of being alive as manifest through the functioning of the body. This experience-near conceptualization is somewhat obfuscated, however, by the link to Primary Process. Winnicott creates a complex model of the True Self that is both somatic and psychic. He also clearly states that the True Self is psychologically primary, at least to begin, and not impacted by external stimuli.

The False Self, on the other hand, appears in Winnicott's writings as a product of early experience. He states that in attempting to understand the "aetiology of the False Self we are examining the stage of first object-relationships" (1960a, p.xx). Bacal (1990) understands the formulation as follows

> Winnicott has suggested that the very core of the self in a healthy person remains isolated from the outside world, that this core is never influenced by external reality, and that the primitive-defenses that the infant erects in reaction to traumatic experiences [the false self] are, above all, intended to prevent this core from being found, altered, or even communicated with. (pp. 263-264)

Schacht (1988) explores Winnicott's (1963) model of the non-communicative self in Winnicott's paper, Communicating and Not Communicating. In that paper, Winnicott elaborates the idea that each person has a private self which is forever silent. He states

> I suggest that in health there is a core to the personality that corresponds to the True Self of the split personality; I suggest that this core never communicates with the world of perceived objects, and that the

individual person knows that it must never be communicated with or be influenced by external reality...each individual is an isolate, permanently non-communicating, permanently unknown, in fact unfound. (p. 187)

From this it is unclear if Winnicott is making a distinction between the non-communicative core of the normative personality and an isolated core that results from the erecting of defenses stemming from impingement.

At an earlier point Winnicott links the core of the personality to the notion of inherited potentials. He states (1960)

> Another phenomenon that needs consideration at this phase is the hiding of the core of the personality. Let us examine the concept of a central or True Self. The central self could be said to be the inherited potential which is experiencing a continuity of being, and acquiring in its own way and at its own speed a personal psychic reality and a personal body-scheme. (p. 46)

Winnicott here states his belief that the isolation of this core is normative in health. He also extends the idea of the primary nature of the True Self by referring to it as an inherited potential.

In all these variations, True self, non-communicative self, and central self, Winnicott attempted to conceptualize the *Self as Core*. This led him to contemplate whether this core self was innate, whether it formed through the defensive action of the False Self, whether it ever had any relational contact, and whether it acted as a template for the potential evolving self.

The Self as Process

In exploring the notion of the self as primary, Winnicott develops several key concepts that offer a theoretical foundation for his thinking. In 1953 he stated that in order for a psychoanalytic theory to adequately account for the workings of the human being it requires some means of understanding symbol formation. He related this problem to Fairbairn's model and notes that, like Melanie Klein, Fairbairn did not have a conceptual vehicle to account for creativity. He writes (1953)

> Fairbairn nowhere states how the infant makes the [theoretical] first object. In his theory, primary psychic creativity is not a human prop-

erty; an infinite series of introjections and projections form the infant's psychic experience. Fairbairn's theory here lines up with the theory given us by Melanie Klein, which also allows no tribute to be paid to the idea of primary psychic creativity. (p. 420)

The problem in Fairbairn's model, according to Winnicott, stems from the need to create an object before one can have a template for introjecting it. He quotes Fairbairn (1952) in support of this as saying, "It is an object which is sought, even if, to be found, it has first to be made" (p. 141). And later in 1968 Winnicott comments on Klein's view

It is possible to use Melanie Klein's emphasis on projection and introjection if at base there is allowed the individual's creative element that must be fundamental for the individual, but which need not be fundamental for the observer. (p. 205)

These ideas on primary creativity and symbol formation link the *Self as Core* to the *Self as Process*. Through positing an innate potential for creativity and an ongoing creative potential, Winnicott forges a system of theoretical support for comprehending the psyche as purposive. These ideas also point the way toward appreciating the link of the Purposive Self to the dream as an expression of that purpose. This link will be further explored in Chapter three on dream theory.

One of Winnicott's earliest formulations for the overlap of *Core* and *Process* was the concept of the 'spontaneous gesture' which formed from his earliest usage of the construct of the self.

In his paper, <u>Clinical Notes on Disorders of Childhood</u> (1931), Winnicott describes a girl who had become depressed and isolated. He states, "Instead of being her own contented *self* she now gets quickly tired of things, losing interest in one toy after another" (in Schacht, 1988, p. 518). In this formulation Winnicott uses the notion of the self to approach the sense of being alive and having an interest in life. By 1960 Winnicott develops this idea further and its link to the True Self. He states (1960a)

Periodically, the infant's gesture gives expression to a spontaneous impulse; the source of this gesture is the True Self, and the gesture indi-

cates the existence of a potential True Self…I have here linked the idea
of the True Self with the spontaneous gesture. (p. 145)

Winnicott had a deep appreciation for the capacity for simply being, and for
the significance of play.

> It is in playing and only in playing that the individual child or adult
> is able to be creative and to use the whole personality. And is only in
> being creative that the individual discovers the self. (1971, p. xx)

For Winnicott, play is the *Process* of the self, revealing the spontaneous gesture, a flow of being, emanating from the core of a person's psyche. Also
important in this conceptualization is the fact that Winnicott appears to be
conceiving of this spontaneous gesture as unprompted by the environment.
For Winnicott, this spontaneous gesture forms the basis for authenticity and
its absence marks the existence of the False Self. He states (1960a)

> In the extreme examples of False Self development, the True Self is
> so well hidden that spontaneity is not a feature in the infant's living
> experiences. Compliance is then the main feature, with imitation as a
> specialty. (p. 147)

And with more clarity he states

> At the earliest stage the True Self is the theoretical position from
> which come the *spontaneous gesture* and the personal idea. The spon-
> taneous gesture is the True Self in action. Only the True Self can be
> creative and only the True Self can feel real. (ibid, p. 148)

Following from the idea that the True Self represents an authentic and creative impulse, comes the notion that this impulse for authenticity is primary.
Winnicott then refers to this as an 'inherited potential'.

> Infants come into *being* differently according to whether the conditions
> are favourable or unfavourable. At the same time conditions do not
> determine the infant's potential. This is inherited, and it is legitimate
> to study this inherited potential of the individual as a separate issue,
> *provided always that it is accepted that the inherited potential of an infant*

> *cannot become the infant unless linked to maternal care.* (1960, p. 43) (italics
> in original)

And in attempting to better understand the nature of this inherited potential
he states in the same article, "The inherited potential includes a tendency
toward growth and development" (p. 43).

For Winnicott, the inherited potential is not only the creative impulse
or the notion of primary creativity, but is also "a tendency toward growth and
development." And it is here that the discussion moves into the domain of the
Self as Process and into a clearer view of the functioning of the Purposive Self.

> The basis of child-development is the physical existence of the infant
> with his or her inherited tendencies. These inherited tendencies in-
> clude the maturational drive to forward development...In more hid-
> den ways there starts in the infant and continues on in the child a
> tendency towards integration of the personality, the word integration
> tending to have more and more complex meaning as time goes on and
> as the child gets older. (1963a, pp. 95-96)

A further elaboration of this comes when he states that the "self...is the
person who is me who is only me who has a totality based on the operation
of the maturational processes" (Schacht, 1988, p. 516). In this way, the authenticity of the person is expressed and furthered through the maturational
processes.

Winnicott built a model of the person with an innate authenticity, the
True Self, that becomes revealed through creative processes, the spontaneous
gesture and the original idea, and is further supported by the maturational
processes that work to make manifest the person that is contained within
this original innate authenticity. In this review of Winnicott's work on the
construct of the self, two central ideas have emerged. 1.) Winnicott brought
the *Self as Person* into greater focus through his emphasis on the relational
impact of the mother in the formation of the self as a unit with boundaries
between the me and the not-me. 2.) He developed his ideas of the *Self as Core*
and the *Self as Process* in order to account for authenticity, innate endowment,
creativity, and the maturational unfolding of the True Self. These efforts by
Winnicott, when viewed through the lens of this essay, represent a significant
contribution to understanding the purposive in human experience. Yet it is

also important to acknowledge that Winnicott never attempted to relate his ideas of primary creativity or maturational processes to the existing Freudian metapsychology, nor did he ever directly apply his ideas of the *Self as Process* to the function of dreaming.

Heinz Kohut

Growing out of ego psychology and the initial formulations of Hartmann (1939, 1948, 1950, 1956), Kohut's contribution to the conceptualization of the self took three primary forms. First, Kohut shifted the focus of American psychoanalysis from the ego to a "psychology in which the self is seen as the centre of the psychological universe" (Kohut, 1977, p. XV). Second, paralleling the developments in Object Relations theory in England, Kohut conceptualized the development of the self as a function of relational/environmental dynamics (Gedo & Goldberg, 1973). Third, Kohut conceived of the self as capable of maintaining a unified cohesion and continuity through "self-generated" processes (Kohut, 1977, p. 139).

Kohut, like Winnicott, was modest in his certainty about the self. He states (1977)

> My investigation contains hundreds of pages dealing with the self—yet it never assigns an inflexible meaning to the term self, it never explains how the essences of the self should be defined. But I admit this without contrition or shame. The self is…not knowable in its essence. (pp. 310-311)

Lachmann (1996) goes farther by when he states that Kohut never defined the self. And Friedland (1978) states that Kohut (and Sullivan) "unnecessarily mystify and becloud the understanding and possible definition of the self" (p. 557). Although there is support for these ideas, they are perhaps oversimplifications. Kohut may have avoided definitions that were foreclosed, but there is a great deal of material from which to infer the ways in which he understood the nature and development of the self.

Frank Faranda

The Self as Person

Forming the basis of Kohut's model of the self is what this essay refers to as the *Self as Person*. In Kohut's (1977) language this is "...a functioning self—a psychological sector in which ambitions, skills, and ideals form an unbroken continuum that permits joyful creative activity" (p. 63). And

> Whenever we are observing a person who strives for pleasure or pursues vengeful or destructive purposes (or who is in conflict concerning these aims or opposes them), it is possible to discern a self which, while it includes drives (and/or defenses) in its organization, has become a supra-ordinated configuration whose significance transcends that of the sum of its parts. (ibid., p 97)

Kohut conceived of the self as the unity that includes elements such as drives, defenses, and conflicts. He also postulated the self as a hypothetical center to the personality, which he termed the nuclear self. Describing the nuclear self in a case formulation, Kohut (1977) writes

> The damage to his nuclear self was widespread. It affected all three of the major constituents of this structure, namely, the two polar areas—the grandiose-exhibitionistic self and the idealized parent imago—and the intermediate area—the executive functions (talents, skills) needed for the realization of the patterns of the basic ambitions and basic ideals that were laid down in the two basic areas. (p. 49)

Kohut here lays out his complex schema for the development and functioning of the *Self as Person*. In Kohut's model, the self consists of three areas: the two poles, and an intermediate area. The origin of the two poles is in part determined by the relational interactions with the environment, but the exact nature of this formation is often difficult to understand due to Kohut's somewhat distant language. Offering some clarification, Kohut (1977) states, "Nuclear ambitions and ideals are the poles of the self" (p. 243). These poles then, are what move the self and what guide the self; in-between these two poles are the executive functions, presumably of the ego. The *Self as Person* in Kohut's model represents the unity of the personality from one pole to the other.

20

Implicit in these formulations of the nuclear self is a relational imperative. Self-object experience, the "mutual empathy" between parent and infant, helps to form this nuclear self and it is through subsequent self-object experiences that the firmness and cohesion of the unified personality is either threatened or maintained.

The Self as Core

Kohut's model of the self contains several formulations on the existence of a core aspect (Friedland, 1978). These formulations include ideas on the innate potential of the self as well as the relational development of the self. Both these views are present in his writings, yet the formulation for understanding the innate aspect of the self is left unfinished (Sutherland, 1993). Bridging both of these ideas Kohut (1977) states

> When, within the matrix of mutual empathy between the infant and his self-object, the baby's innate potentialities and the self-object's expectations with regard to the baby converge. It is permissible to consider this juncture the point of origin of the infant's primal, rudimentary self. (p. 99)

And

> The nuclear self, in particular, is not formed via conscious encouragement and praise and via conscious discouragement and rebuke, but by the deeply anchored responsiveness of the self-objects, which in the last analysis, is a function of the self-objects' own nuclear selves. (ibid. p. 100)

Expressing the other perspective, Kohut (1977) goes on to conceive of the self in infancy as a biological given.

> May we then not speak of a self in statu nescendi even at a time when the infant in isolation—a psychological artifact—can be looked upon only as a biological unit? (ibid., p. 100)

Also in support of the innate aspect of self are Kohut's use of expressions such as "talents," and "intrinsic potentialities," as well as his use of the term "virtual self" (p. 101) in describing the early self of the infant prior to achieving

21

integration, cohesion, and boundaries through internalization processes connected with self-object relations. Supporting the necessity of both perspectives, Kohut (1977) holds that empathy is "the most important way in which the child's *innate potentialities* are selectively nourished or thwarted" (p. 100, italics mine).

Returning to the question of understanding Kohut's view on the origin and nature of his innate, "virtual self," Sutherland (1993) believes that Kohut was reluctant to formulate a theory of self "with biological roots" (p. 15) due to the metapsychological implications.

The Self as Process

The *Self as Process* in Kohut's work is found primarily in the establishment and maintenance of cohesion and self-unity (Gedo, & Goldberg, 1973; Lachmann, 1996). Related to this process, Kohut (1977) writes

> the success of the analysis is measured primarily by evaluating the cohesion and firmness of the self and, above all, by deciding whether one sector of the self has become continuous from one of its poles to the other, and has become the reliable initiator and performer of joyful undertaken activities. (p. 134)

In discussing the psychopathology related to this process Kohut goes on to say

> The essential psychopathology in the narcissistic personality disorders is defined by the fact that the self has not been solidly established, that its cohesion and firmness depend on the presence of a self-object (on the development of a self-object transference), and that it responds to the loss of the self-object with simple enfeeblement, various regressions, and fragmentation. (p. 137)

Kohut is giving voice to an important question related to his formulation for the *Self as Process:* is the use of self objects part of normative functioning throughout life, or is it only required when the self lacks cohesion? In reference to this question

> I have never claimed that the formulations of ego psychology are wrong or useless. I have only claimed that they do not allow us to formulate

in a satisfactory way those crucial attributes of the psyche *as it moves toward health: the capacity for self-soothing, the sense of continuity of the self in time,* and the crucial role of the self-object in providing the opportunity for the acquisition of these attributes. (1984, italics mine, p. 65)

Kohut refers to the processes that move the individual toward health as "crucial attributes of the psyche" and clearly indicates that these attributes are determined by the relational influence of the self-object. But one wonders, following Sutherland (1993), whether Kohut's ability to construct a model for an innate biological process of cohesion, was hampered by the metapsychological implications of such a model. In other words, would Kohut have needed to postulate a separate drive or energy source independent of libido and narcissism in order to fully support the independent functioning of the maintenance of the self?

From Freud to Kohut: A Mid-point Review

One of the primary characteristics observable in the theory of the self beginning with Freud and continuing to Kohut was the clear increase in the weight given to relational influences in the development of the self. The self of Winnicott and Kohut was clearly more relationally determined than the self of Freud and Hartmann. A second characteristic growing out of the first was the theoretical struggle to maintain contact with notions that could account for the biological, innate, or primary origins of the self. In relation to the first characteristic, this translates into the dichotomy of nature vs. nurture. At times this pursuit of what constitutes nature in the formation of the self took the form of an understanding of the instinctual basis for the self (Hartmann, 1939), the existence of primary narcissism (Freud, 1915, Kohut, 1971), primary creativity (Winnicott, 1971), innate potentials (Hartmann, 1950), or inherited tendencies (Winnicott, 1960). A third characteristic of the self in the majority of theories during this time period was the broad conceptualization of the self as a unity. This revealed itself in all three domains. In terms of the *Self as Person,* most theorists, (with the exception of Sullivan who will be discussed later in this chapter) hold the clinical and theoretical impression of the self as a unity. Even in the work of Winnicott on the split between True and False Selves there is the overarching notion of the self as representative of the wholeness of the personality and as contained in the body as a unit self. In terms of the *Self as Core,* this implicit unity translates into a model of a centered self with an essence or innate given. The formation of this core, it can be argued, was always troublesome to psychoanalytic theory. Was this core purely innate or was it an innate "potential" activated by the environment? For the most part, these ideas of the core of the self remained nascent, unclear, and often paradoxical as seen in the writings of Winnicott and Kohut. In the domain of the *Self as Process,* the notion of unity translated into ideas whereby tendencies, functions, or forces are working for synthesis of the personality or cohesion of the self. In these models, the self is envisioned to be working continually toward maintaining itself as an integrated yet evolving unit.

The conceptualizations of the self that were developed out of Ego Psychology, Object Relations, and Self Psychology in the 1950s, 1960s, and 1970s have continued to exert tremendous influence on subsequent generations of clinicians. Followers of Hartmann, Winnicott, and Kohut have maintained basic adherence to the central notions of the self developed by their founders and have also extended the theories to embrace more recent thinking (Model, 1976; Lachmann, 1996). In this way, these ideas have not ceased to exist, but have endured with change.

Shifts in the Underlying Paradigm

In the late 1970s, several shifts in the underlying theoretical, philosophical, and cultural fabric converged to bring about the possibility for a new underlying theory of the self. The collapse of Freud's metapsychology and the emergence of postmodernism together with advances in infant observational techniques and neurobiological understanding of infancy necessitated alterations in the understanding of the self (Gedo, 1997). Philosophically, these ideas grew out of deconstructionism, hermeneutics, and social constructivism. Clinically, they translated into conceptions of the self that included a primary decentering of subjectivity (Bromberg, 1991, 1993, 1996); a relativization of the importance of history (Schaefer, 1999); a heightened regard for the experience of the present moment (Greenberg & Mitchell, 1983); and an awareness that authenticity, meaning, and truth are at best a subjective experience, and at worst, an illusion (Hoffmann, 1992).

From Sullivan to Bromberg: the Illusion of Self

The most profound changes in the conceptualization of the self that were wrought by postmodernism and the collapse of Freud's metapsychology can be seen in the work of Bromberg (1991, 1993, 1996) on the multiplicity of the self. These conceptualizations primarily impact an understanding of the *Self as Person,* but also approach ideas of the *Self as Core* and the *Self as Process.*

Bromberg's views on the multiplicity of the self grew out of the relational tradition inaugurated by Sullivan (Bromberg, 1993). As Frederickson, (2000) states, "postmodern and relational schools of psychoanalysis have been greatly influenced by Sullivan's constructivist concept of the self" (p. 587). Frederickson goes on to state that Sullivan "exploded the myth of a person as a single self, thereby anticipating the postmodernist movement" (p. 587). Sullivan, however, appears to have been most influenced by what Friedland (1978) refers to as logical positivism. And as Friedland goes on to say, it was this logical positivism that made it difficult for Sullivan to theorize about the self. In reviewing Sullivan (1938, 1940) what appears to have been difficult for Sullivan was not theorizing about the self, but theorizing about anything that was not directly observable (Mullahy, 1945). As Sullivan himself states, "The unique individuality of the other fellow need never concern us as scientists" (p. 12). And earlier, Sullivan (1938) writes, "It [the self] is made manifest in interpersonal situations and not otherwise" (p. 121). Mullahy (1945), a close follower of Sullivan, makes clear Sullivan's views on the nature of the self

> The self-system is *the limit,* the containing matrix of the 'me-you patterns.' Furthermore, the personality, the hypothetical entity postulated in order to make all one's behavior intelligible, is the limit of the self-system. (p. 134)

And

> ...he [Sullivan] seems to be emphasizing the fact that a person is not an isolated entity, that personality is revealed and has its being in interpersonal relations, and is observable only in such interpersonal relations. (p. 146)

Mullahy (1945) goes on to state that Sullivan found the term, individuality, objectionable. Individuality as a psychological construct evokes the idea of the existence of an innate substance or quality of a person that exists in its own right, something related to the *Self as Core*. Mullahy (1945) notes further that one of the motivations of Sullivan for denying the existence of a "unique individuality" was to avoid recourse to archaic religious conceptions. He states

> Traditionally, the soul is a unique spiritual entity or substance, which can subsist independently. Some people talk about individuality as if it were literally a spiritual essence. (p. 146)

Instead, for Sullivan, the person we experience as our self is formed from the pattern of interpersonal interactions; the self in this model is essentially "an illusion." Lesser (1978) sums up the ideas of Sullivan on the self when she states "Sullivan held that there is no self apart from an empirical self which develops as a product of actual interpersonal relations" (p. 547).

What appears most important to note regarding Sullivan is that his work both paralleled and differed from the efforts of others working during the same period. Like Fromm and Horney, Sullivan emphasized the importance of interpersonal relations, but unlike these contemporaries, Sullivan restricted his view to what was directly observable: the manifestations of self in relationship. Horney and Fromm, on the other hand, while stressing the importance of relationship and the conflict with culture, each had views of the self as authentic, original, and as a true potentiality of the individual (Lesser, 1978).

Bromberg (1993, 1996) takes the work of Sullivan on the relational basis for self together with social constructivist ideas and builds a model of personality in which self-states, multiple and imminently dissociable, replace a model in which the self is viewed as unified, with an innate component, and a functional cohesion. In conceptualizing his view of the structure of the mind, Bromberg (1993) states

> Freud's view of consciousness and unconsciousness is embedded in the idea of a self or psyche that is inherently unitary and structured archeologically in terms of a particular layer's degree of access to awareness; thus, we find his topographical conceptions of conscious, preconscious,

and unconscious. I do not suggest that these distinctions have been lost or that they are not worthwhile. My argument, rather, is that we are moving increasingly in the direction of a model in which our view of what is conscious and what is unconscious is informed by a conception of the mind as a nonlinear, dialectical process of meaning construction, organized by the equilibrium between stability and growth of one's self-representation—the balance between the need to preserve meaning (the ongoing experience of 'being oneself') and the need to construct new meaning in the service of relational adaptation that Sullivan (1940) called *interpersonal adaptive success.* (pp. 149-150)

And with regard to the changing psychoanalytic field, Bromberg (1996) believes that

[an increasing number of contemporary analysts] now share the clinical observation that…even in the most well-functioning individual, normal personality structure is shaped by dissociation as well as by repression and intrapsychic conflict…parallel with this development, a discernable shift has been taking place with regard to psychoanalytic understanding of the human mind and the nature of unconscious mental processes…away from the idea of a conscious/preconscious/unconscious distinction per se, toward a view of the self as decentered, and the mind as a configuration of shifting, non-linear, discontinuous states of consciousness in an ongoing dialectic with the healthy illusion of unitary selfhood. (p. 512)

Related to the constructivist and relational model, Bromberg (1993) also believes that "The clinical focus is not as much on discovering past roots of current problems…as on exploring the way in which the self-states comprising a patient's personal identity are linked to each other, to the external world, and to the past, present and future" (p. 150).

For Bromberg (1993), personality growth is not a matter of replacing a maladaptive self representation with a healthy self representation, but "a process of addressing individual subnarratives, each on its own terms, and enabling negotiation to take place between them" (p. 161). By subnarratives, Bromberg is referring to "a set of discrete, typically overlapping schemata of who he [a person] is, and that each is organized around a particular self-other

configuration that is held together by a uniquely powerful affective state"
(pp. 161-162). He goes on to say (1993)

> To put it as simply as possible, I argue that there is no such thing as
> an integrated self—a 'real you.' Self-expression and human relatedness
> will inevitably collide...this is what I believe *self-acceptance* means and
> what *creativity* is really all about—the capacity to feel like one self
> while being many. (p. 166)

Related to the feeling of being one while being many, Bromberg, (1996)
writes

> When all goes well developmentally, a person is only dimly or mo-
> mentarily aware of the existence of self-states and their respective re-
> alities, because each functions as part of a healthy illusion of cohesive
> personal identity—an overarching cognitive and experiential state felt
> as 'me.' Each self-state is a piece of a functional whole. (p. 514)

Although it is clear that Bromberg denies the existence of a unified
self, there is in the above quote a paradoxical reference to the 'functional
whole'. What isn't clear is the difference for Bromberg between a functional
whole self and an actual whole self. For wholeness, in any model of the mind,
can never truly be more than a usable construct.

The Need for Infant Developmental and Neurobiological Theory

From the above picture of the postmodern perspective on the multiplicity of the self, it becomes clear that concepts such as uniqueness, a central
element in any model of the *Self as Core,* and integration, a central element in
any model of the *Self as Process,* become problematic and philosophically contentious. Without theoretical principles such as psychic energy and inherited
biological givens, it is difficult to build a model of a psychological process
such as cohesion, or a model of a core aspect of the personality such as a True
Self. The lack of credibility attributed to Freud's original notions of psychic
energy and inherited potentials makes it increasingly difficult to formulate
models in these domains (Gedo, 1999). Authors such as Klein (1976), Schaefer
(1976), Rosenblatt and Thikstun (1970), Holt (1989), and Rubenstein (1997)

have all illustrated the ways in which Freud's metapsychological principles are erroneous and experience distant.

Specific to the domain of the *Self as Process*, Rubenstein (1997) has shown that the concept of psychic energy is not a valid biological concept and as Gedo (1999) states "its use in psychoanalytic theory thus amounts to resort to a vitalist notion" (p. 200). Also invalid from the postmodern perspective are the concepts of integration and cohesion. Since there is no unified self, there is no need to postulate a process to maintain it. Thus, as postmodernism began to gain influence and as Freud's metapsychology began to be dismantled, the possibility of formulating notions of the *Self as Process* became more difficult within the existing framework.

To fill this gap, psychodynamic theory has turned its attention to the work of theorists and researchers in infant development and neurobiology. These contributions, such as those of Stern (1985), Emde (1983), Schore (1994) and Tronick (1989), offer a potential model to replace what was lost through the dismantling of Freud's metapsychology and the influence of postmodernism (Gedo, 1997, 1999).

Affect Regulation and the Self as Process

Theories on affect regulation and the formation of the self became explicit in developmental, neurobiological, and psychoanalytic literature during the past 20 years. This emergence of interest in the self as primarily a regulatory phenomenon had as its impetus changes in the understanding of early infant experience as well as changes in several general concepts of psychoanalysis that rest upon understandings of infancy. These areas of interest include primary narcissism, affiliative instincts, ego capacities at birth, autism and symbiosis, preverbal levels of communication, affect as an organizing principle, and the importance of the mother in the development of the child. Recent developmental theories work to fill the void left by the absence of a valid concept for psychic energy and the shaky metapsychological foundation for any concept related to integration, synthesis, or maturation. In this way, the concept of affect replaces that of psychic energy and drive. As Emde (1983) states, "Our central nervous system is constructed in such a way that all experience is affective...it provides incentives for developmental goals." (p. 173)

Frank Faranda

The actual neurophysiological processes of affect regulation are extensively detailed by Schore (1994, 1997). He states (1997)

> In early development an adult provides much of the necessary modulation of infant states, especially after a state disruption and across a transition between states, and this allows for the development of self-regulation. (p. 16)

In this process, repair is central to the structuring activity in the growing brain of the infant. Schore (1997) tells us that the alteration between states of disregulation and regulation are important in helping the infant to internalize a self-regulatory function. This notion is also found in the work of Tronick (1989, 1998) where the process of interactive repair of failed attunement is central in *brain-to-brain* affect regulation.

> This recovery mechanism underlies the phenomenon of 'interactive' repair in which participation of the caregiver is responsible for the reparation of dyadic misstatements. (Tronick, 1989, p. 16)

From a neurological perspective, Schore quotes Diamond et al. (1963) as conceptualizing that the caregiver provides an 'auxiliary cortex' to the infant. This is very similar to ideas of the caregiver supplying an auxiliary ego or self to the infant. It is also similar to the self-object work of Kohut in stating that the infant/child/adult uses the object for maintenance of the self. Schore (1997) states, "In these transactions she is downloading programs from her brain into the infant's brain" and "[the brain's] growth literally requires brain-brain interaction and occurs in the context of a positive affective relationship between mother and infant" (p. 19-20).

Relational influences, in these models, are seen to be the source of the regulatory functions which become internalized during early infancy. What is primary within the self is not the function of regulation, but the potential for the function of regulation.

Emde's Prerepresentational Core
Emde (1983) states initially that the idea of a prerepresentational self seems to be a contradiction. "How can there be a self before the development of a mental capacity for representation" (p. 165)? Emde, however, goes on to

30

postulate a center of the self he refers to as the *core self*. For Emde, this core self is a relational aspect of the self that is preverbal and affective in nature, forming through the first interactions with the mother. This affective core, according to Emde, guarantees the continuity of experience over all the changes in our person. It also guarantees that we understand other human beings. Emde (1983) goes on to state, "Finally because our affective core touches upon those aspects of experience which are most important to us as individuals, it also allows us to get in touch with the uniqueness of our own (and others) uniqueness" (p. 180). Emde's understanding of a person's uniqueness is not an invariant or a biological inheritance, rather, it is the internalization of the earliest affective exchanges with the primary caregiver.

> Biologically based principles are species-general, yet through their functioning they seem to assure individuality...because of man's complexity and the fact that no two individuals are born the same, the general biological principles of self-regulation, social-fittedness, and affective monitoring work toward the coherent uniqueness of each developing person. Thus it seems a paradoxical truth of self that our heritage guarantees both our species-wide commonness and our individual uniqueness. (Emde, 1983, p. 179)

The question of uniqueness, whether biological, relational, or an interaction of both, presents psychology with one of its greatest challenges. As Emde (1983) asks, "How can we change so much and yet we know we are the same" (p. 179)?

Conclusion

The construct of the self in psychoanalytic theory has gone through a number of changes beginning with Freud's *das ich*. These changes represented significant alterations in the way in which psychoanalysis conceptualized the model of the mind, the course of development, and the nature of purposiveness in the psyche. These alterations have paralleled several major shifts in the essential fabric of psychoanalytic culture; principle among these is the increased emphasis on relational dynamics as a means of explaining the origin, formation, and maintenance of the self without metapsychology or metaphysics. This evolution took many forms in the hands of psychoanalytic theorists such as Winnicott, Kohut, Sullivan, and Bromberg leading to the

31

most recent innovations where the idea of an innate aspect of the *Self as Core* is almost non-existent.

The *Self as Process* in recent theory is understood as a similarly internalized process of affect regulation. As was seen, this shift in the model of the self was due to an interaction of forces including the movement to the relational, the collapse of Freud's metapsychology, and the rise of postmodernism. These influences have made it increasingly difficult to formulate ideas for a Purposive Self. As Winnicott (1953) noted, a comprehensive psychoanalytic theory of the mind needs to be able to account for symbol formation, primary creativity, and the innate maturational forces. These are the manifestations of the *Self as Process* and it is the work of this essay to explore ways in which these ideas can be accounted for within the context of contemporary theory. Most significant of these manifestations, however, and the area where the Purposive Self can be seen most clearly, is in the realm of the dreaming mind.

Chapter Three: The Dreaming Mind

From the earliest days of Freud's speculations into the workings of the mind, the dream has held a prominent yet precarious position in psychoanalytic treatment. It has been both a guide to new theoretical discoveries and an anchor to existing theory. It has been exalted and vilified, looked on with suspicion and trusted, seen as a message and as a dubious blip of mentation. It has been a defense, a revelation, a disguise, an integrator of personality, a problem solver, an evacuative mechanism, a royal road, and an annoying bit of pathology. Yet through all the vicissitudes in sentiment and alterations in understanding, the dream has continued to be dreamed.

Speculations on dream function and formation have the capacity both to deepen and to alter our understandings of the mind. Arlow and Brenner (1964) state

> ...according to Freud, one of the tasks of a theory of the mind, if it is to be considered a satisfactory theory, is to make clear to us the place which dreams and dreaming occupy in mental life with respect to other mental phenomena. (p. 143)

From this point of view, any theory of the mind should account for the dream in a way similar to Freud's comprehensive model. Looking at the Irma dream, Freud uncovered a latent meaning quite distinct from the manifest dream, and asked, *what must the mind be like if it deceives itself* (Lansky, 1992). Out of this question, Freud built his initial topographical model of the mind as outlined in The Interpretation of Dreams (TIOD). In that model, the dream was understood using the basic principles of psychoanalytic theory. Interpretation of the dream was equivalent with psychoanalytic process and the place of the dream in treatment was integral.

Joining the ideas put forth in Chapter Two for the *Self as Process,* together with the idea of a link between the function and formation of the dream and the essential workings of the mind, this chapter will explore dream theory as road to better understanding the nature of the mind that produces the dream. When approached from this perspective, the dream will point to an underlying model of the mind with a functional capability equivalent to what this essay refers to as the Purposive Self.

The focus of this exploration will center on the relationship of dream interpretation to dream theory. Specifically, attention will rest on the theoretical implications of the observable shift in dream interpretation toward an appreciation and acceptance of the manifest level of the dream. This shift in the clinical use of the dream was effected without a specific dream theory to explain why the manifest dream should be viewed as meaningful. It is here postulated that this phenomenon, the separation of dream interpretation from dream theory, has impacted psychoanalytic theory and psychodynamic treatment in two important ways:

1.) The clinical use of dreams in psychodynamic treatment has become less important and less prominent because there isn't a clear theory to support interpretive methods.

2.) Psychoanalytic understandings of the workings of the mind have remained unexamined in a specific area, the *Self as Process*, because theorists have not attempted to extrapolate a model of the mind from the clinical acknowledgement that the manifest dream is a meaningful communication. In other words, contemporary psychoanalysis is failing to ask, *what must the mind be like if it **does not deceive itself?***

Three areas related to the dream in psychoanalytic theory will be explored in the remainder of this chapter. The prominence of the dream in early models of treatment will be contrasted with the current decline in use of dream interpretation. Following this will be a study of the ways in which the use of the dream has shifted from a view of the manifest dream as a disguise to a view of the manifest dream as a figurative representation. Through this, it will be seen that this shift toward the manifest was not accompanied by a change in dream theory. The final question that this chapter will ponder is: what implications arise from the lack of dream theory? And most important, is our clinical theory less effective without the ability to conceptualize the dream as a manifestation of the Purposive Self?

The Prominence of the Dream

Many believe that without the dream there would have been no psychoanalysis (Freud, 1924; Greenson, 1970; Lansky, 1992; Lippmann, 2000).

The link of the dream to the fabric of psychoanalytic theory took shape through Freud's (1900) work <u>The Interpretation of Dreams</u> (TIOD). Freud himself (1924) states

> Psychoanalysis, may be said to have been born with the twentieth century; for the publication in which it emerged before the world as something new—my Interpretation of Dreams—bears the date 1900. (p.191)

In TIOD, Freud not only outlines a model of dream interpretation and dream theory, but also establishes a model of the mind, a model of psychopathology, and a model of treatment. TIOD is often viewed as a textbook of psychoanalytic theory and not simply a model for the interpretation of dreams (Lansky, 1992). The primary importance of this link between dream theory and clinical theory is that Freud was able to achieve a meaningful method for understanding the function and formation of the dream that simultaneously uncovered the workings of the mind. This integration of dream theory with clinical theory is one of the primary differences between the place of the dream in the past and the place of the dream today. And as stated, a goal of this essay is to reestablish a theoretical consistency.

In 1900, Freud stated, "the interpretation of dreams is the royal road to a knowledge of the unconscious activities of the mind" (1900, p. 608). He understood dream theory and TIOD as his "sheet-anchor" during the early days of psychoanalysis when he was so full of doubt (Grubrich-Simitis, 2000). He described TIOD as the "foundation stone of psychoanalysis" (Freud, 1913, p. 170). It was a text that changed a field of study and shifted what was once simply a psychotherapeutic method into a general depth psychology (Grubrich-Simitis, 2000). Freud edited the book eight times during his life (Greenson, 1970); the importance of this work for Freud cannot be overestimated.

Likewise, the earliest adherents to psychoanalysis shared Freud's enthusiasm for TIOD, exhibited a clear allegiance to Freud's model, and were reluctant to offer emendations. Lippmann (2000) sums this up by stating, "It could be said that dreams were the heart and soul of psychoanalysis from its very inception" (p. 627). And due to this equivalence, it was impossible to conduct an analysis during the early years without dreams.

Freud made three explicit statements on dreams in works other than TIOD. These contributions restated or amended dream theory and its relation to the metapsychology. The first of these after TIOD was in 1916, in The Metapsychological Supplement to the Theory of Dreams. Following this came The Introductory Lectures on Psychoanalysis, in 1917 and the final formal work on dreams in 1933, The Revision of the Theory of Dreams. It can be said that these additional works were attempts by Freud to solidify, rather than change his theory.

The Place of the Dream: The Early Phase

The first signs of the decline in prominence of the dream within psychoanalytic theory were noted by Freud in 1933. He also noted that interest in dream interpretation had fallen into decline.

> In the earlier volumes [of the International Journal] you will find a recurrent section heading, 'On Dream Interpretation' containing numerous contributions on various points in the theory of dreams. But the further you go, the rarer these contributions become, and finally the sectional heading disappears completely. (1933, p. 33)

And in a jocular tone he adds, "analysts act as though they have nothing more to say about dreams" (ibid, p. 33).

The Place of the Dream: The Middle Phase

The trends that Freud observed in 1933 continued and by the 1950s, with the developments of Ego Psychology and the shift from unconscious wish to structural conflict, the dream's position within clinical practice became further compromised. Many theorists held that the dream was no longer a privileged element in an analysis, but an element like any other (Lorand, 1956; Waldhorn, 1967). During this period several studies and conferences were established to explore the dream in relation to general psychoanalytic theory. Lorand (1956) was the published account of one such conference and many noted clinicians such as L. Rangell participated. Rangell, (in Lorand 1956), states, "As psychoanalysis expands and becomes more inclusive and complex, the dream shrinks to a relatively lesser place alongside the many more peripheral and subtle and varied phenomena which come now within its sphere of interest" (p. 135).

Striking a somewhat different note, Friedman (1957) states, "The current revival of interest in the dream as well as the publication of quite a number of excellent textbooks and monographs on the subject has served to highlight the fact that many problems of dream psychology have yet to be solved, and that detailed studies of specific dream problems are needed" (p. 363).

In 1967 the Kris Study Group published its four-year findings in Waldhorn (1967). The impetus for this study group was the already noted revival of interest in dreams as well as the work of Arlow and Brenner (1964) in modifying dream theory to better reflect the changes initiated by the structural model. Waldhorn (1967) notes that there were no mutually agreed upon reference points for understanding the clinical material of dreams, no theoretical common ground. The Kris Study group also noted that during the period of 1923—1963 the dream was neglected, and instead work went into other areas. Most notable of these areas was the transference. The overall finding of the Kris Study Group with regard to the position of the dream was that many analysts at that time leaned toward the idea that the dream was no longer a special element in a psychoanalytic treatment (Lansky, 1992).

Brenner (1969) expresses a contrary view of the dream as still important to an understanding of unconscious mental processes when he states, "dream analysis is, generally speaking, outstandingly the *best* method for learning about unconscious mental processes" (p. 210), and, "Dreams and their interpretation still occupy a special place in our minds—our professional minds—whether we acknowledge it or not" (p. 198). But at the end of his article he equivocates slightly by stating, "Other consequences of inner conflicts are as important to analyze as are dreams and may, on occasion, be quite as useful a road to the understanding of a patient's inner conflicts, of his unconscious mind, as a dream would be" (p. 211).

The Place of the Dream: The Recent Phase

Regarding the place of the dream in contemporary psychodynamic treatment, Lansky (1992) asks, "Is the dream still the royal road to the unconscious or just a historically early and somewhat fascinating item of psychoanalytic research?" (p. 10). By way of answering this question he states, "only in the context of the analytic process does the specialness emerge" (p.

10). He does, however, echo the notion that many analysts no longer attribute any specialness to the dream (Lansky, 1992).

In response to the end of the first one hundred years of psychoanalytic dream theory, Lippmann, (2000) notes that in the then most recent meeting of Division 39 of the APA (1999) there was only one paper on dreams. He states, "It is clear that interest in dreams and their interpretation, within psychoanalysis, has significantly diminished over the last past half century" (p. 627).

Understanding the Decline in Position

The range of ideas cited in the literature for understanding the decline in the prominence of the dream extend from the theoretical to the personal. The first idea to be considered is the question of what impact the structural theory had upon the use of the dream. Greenson (1970) and Waldhorn (1967) hold that because Freud's dream theory was built in intimate connection with the topographical model, the change to the structural view depotentiated the theory of the dream. Several authors, including Freud in his 1933 introduction, believe it was the very magnitude of TIOD that discouraged attempts at emulation or elaboration (Waldhorn, 1967; Curtis & Sachs, 1976; Fordham, 1984). Lippmann (2000) argues that there are many reasons to be found for the decline in interest in the dream, but central to these is the therapist's own ambivalence to dreams. He also notes that considerations such as time limits in treatment, level of pathology, frequency of visits, and the need to focus on other aspects of the relationship are also important in understanding the decline. But primary for Lippmann (2000) is the foreclosing certitude of the classical model. According to Lippmann, it was this certitude about the meaning of the dream, a repressed infantile sexual wish, that ultimately caused the dream to lose its vitality in treatment.

Also noted in the literature is the belief that the decline of the dream was due to a change in the goals of psychoanalytic work (Arlow & Brenner, 1964; Curtis & Sachs 1976). In the early days, the goal, according to Arlow and Brenner, was to "arrive at an understanding of the patient's unconscious sexual wishes as quickly as possible…and the dream was the royal road to the unconscious" (p. 140). Blum, (in Curtis & Sachs, 1976) states similarly that the dream has lost its importance in much the same way as hypnosis before it.

A thesis of this essay expands upon the above understandings for the decline of the dream in psychodynamic treatment by exploring the possibility that the current decline is due to the inability of dream theory to remain integrated with clinical theory. In other words, there is no psychological construct in the contemporary psychoanalytic model of the mind to account for the function and formation of the dream, and without the support of a psychological dream theory clinicians lose the conceptual strength that comes from understanding what produces the dream, what organizes the dream work, and for what purpose. As with all clinical material, dream interpretation is dependent upon an internal consistency between model of the mind, model of psychopathology, model of development, and model of treatment.

Zane (1971) reports somewhat pessimistically on a five-year study group aimed at clarifying the diversity of interpretative methods and improving the ability of analysts from different theoretical schools to communicate with one another. Zane reports

> Five years of determined effort to resolve some of our differences has certainly produced no such wondrous integration. In my view the persistence of such differences for so long may well signify something fundamentally wrong with how we psychologists work with dreams. (p. 175)

Regarding the indeterminateness of dream use, Pontalis, (quoted in Curtis & Sachs, 1976) states, "among the major theories of psychoanalysis, the theory of dreams has changed the least, although the dream is variously seen as a message, a puzzle to be deciphered or an intrapsychic experience" (p. 343). What this points to is the un-theoretical use of dreams and the lack of revisions to a model of dream theory.

Most of the major revisions to Freud's psychoanalytic model, Object Relations, Self Psychology, and contemporary relational theory, do not have a model with specific functioning responsible for the production of the dream. Examples of major theorists who have not developed a model to account for the dream are Klein, Winnicott, Fairbairn, and Kohut (the self-state dream of Kohut is never explained in terms of a source, it simply exists). Ego psychologists have theories for the formation of the dream but this is due to their allegiance to Freud's original disguise/wish model.

Several current theorists are attempting to elaborate the functioning of the dream from within existing models yet stopping short of conceptualizing the inner working of dream function and formation. One of the most notable is James Fosshage. Fosshage has written quite extensively on the dream (1983, 1997, 2000) and holds the dream in high regard. He states (1983) that "there is no theoretical necessity to posit the ubiquitous operation of disguise and transformation of latent into manifest content" (p. 257). And regarding his view of dreams he states, "they [dreams] have been insufficiently recognized for their primary developmental, regulatory, conflict-resolving, and reorganizational functions, a role of even greater import than previously conceived" (p. 264). Fosshage believes that the tendency to view the dream as regressive has obscured from view the more synthetic functions of the dream. He states (1983)

> It is my thesis that this metapsychological view of dreams as predominantly a product of regression to primitive-infantile levels of functioning and organization has tended to preclude the recognition of the organizational or synthesizing purposes of the dream, the manifestation of varying levels of organization in dreams, and the use of dream of the assessment of object-relational development or the level of differentiation and structuralization of self and object representations. (p. 252)

A second lineage of theorists who are currently providing rich new considerations for understanding the dream are those theorists that follow Klein and Bion. Most notable of these in relation to dream theory is James Grotstein who has recently published <u>Who Is the Dreamer Who Dreams the Dream</u> (2000). Grotstein expresses his awe at the dream as a creative product, impressive because of the scope of what is being weaved together to form the dream. He speaks to this ability when he states

> It occurred to me that the production of a dream is a unique and mysterious event, an undertaking that requires an ability to think and to create that is beyond the capacity of conscious human beings. As I began to think along this line, I became dissatisfied with Freud's explanation that it is the dream work (the primary process) that creates dreams. (p. 4)

Grotstein adds

> Dreams are dramatic narratives written, directed, and produced by
> a composite dreamer who is unknown to us, who employs narrative
> as the instrument of phantasy and myth and uses Neurophysiologi-
> cal perception—namely visualization—to organize the chaotic frag-
> mented accretions of mental pain left over as residues of yet one more
> day of existence. (p. 10)

In this conceptualization there is the awareness that the dream is highly complex, requiring a multitude of functioning on a multitude of levels and that
this process is beyond the conscious ability of the human ego.

Also a part of this legacy, Donald Meltzer (1984) following Bion, believes
that Freud trivialized the dream by calling it the guardian of sleep. According
to Meltzer, Freud's model was too much dependent upon neurobiological origins and the topographical model. Meltzer has a real love of the dream (Fordham, 1984). He views the dream as a form of thinking (Meltzer, 1984).

Hannah Segal (1983), also following Bion, conceptualizes the dream as a
form of thinking referred to as the alpha function (Bion, 1959). This function
relates to the way in which beta elements, primary elements of experience,
and O, the experience of the unknowable, are transformed into digestible
psychic experience. Segal develops these ideas further by conceptualizing the
dream as an evacuative process in which indigestible elements are projected
away from the self through the dream.

Bollas (1987), another theorist who had a theoretical orientation that
was capable of perceiving the dream in ways that expand the Freudian model,
believes that the Freudian view of the dream as merely a veiled communication has resulted in "neglect of the dream as lived experience" (Bollas, 1987,
p. 64). To Bollas the dream can never be totally known. It is an opportunity
to encounter the unknown other. Bollas shares Grotstein's appreciation for
the dramatic/communicative nature of the dream. He states, "The dream text
is a primordial fiction. What Freud discovered and then neglected was the
notion of the dream space as a night theatre involving the subject in a vivid
re-acquaintance with the Other" (p. 68). And further, "However fruitful the
theoretical contributions of Chapter 7 of The Interpretation of Dreams have
been to psychoanalytic metapsychology, they have obscured the aesthetic discovery of the dream space as theatre" (p. 68). Bollas holds that through the

41

dream one encounters "the unthought known which refers to the unrepressed unconscious" (p. 70).

James Weiss (1986) offers an innovative approach while maintaining allegiance to certain concepts from Ego Psychology. For Weiss, the ego produces dreams to deal with its problems including those that arise from the id. He views the dream as part of self-preservation. In terms of the function of dreams as attempts at problem solving, Weiss states, "The dreams...as already noted, perform their functions whether or not the dreamer is able to consciously interpret them" (p. 225). In this there is the view that the dream is not only problem solving, but psychically reparative as well.

Thomas Ogden, a descendent of the Klein/Winnicott line incorporates the use of dreams into his relational approach to the analytic third. Ogden (1986) views the dream as a communication from one aspect of the self to another aspect of the self. Initially, the process begins as a dream presentation which Ogden views as a product of primary process. After this, he postulates that the dream becomes dreaming in a space that Winnicott (1953) referred to as potential space. It is there that fantasy becomes imagination and the dream becomes dreaming. He proposes that the dream must undergo a transformation in dream space for it to become symbolic dreaming.

Some years later, Ogden (1997) adds the idea of the intersubjective analytic third—the co-created space between patient and analyst—to the experience of the dream. He states, "I shall attempt to explore the implications of the idea that a dream dreamt in the course of an analysis represents a manifestation of the Intersubjective Analytic Third" (1997, p. 139). In this way, Ogden proposes that the dream in this context does not just belong to the patient but is the product of both patient and analyst. It is a joint construction "arising from the interplay of the unconscious of the analyst and the unconscious of the analysand" (p. 142). He also believes it is meaningful to not be able to interpret a dream. He states, "Dreaming (or Dream-life) is a specific form of human experience that cannot be translated into a linear, verbally symbolized narrative without losing touch with the effect created by the dream experience itself, the experience of the dreaming as opposed to the meaning of the dream" (1997, p. 153).

Thus far, three clear tendencies, with a number of exceptions, have been observed in the initial overview of the history of psychoanalytic dream interpretation. One, it has been established that the dream has lost its prominence in psychodynamic treatment; two, dream interpretation has generally shifted to a non-associational use of the manifest content; and three, dream interpretation is no longer supported by a theory that integrates the function and formation of the dream with the basic symbolic functioning of the mind. It has been postulated that there is a correlation between the decline in the position of the dream in treatment and the lack of theoretical support for an interpretive method.

What remains to be explored is the process by which clinicians arrived at the practice of using the manifest dream as a meaningful unit of communication. Through this exploration it will be seen that the evolution in interpretative methods toward the manifest began with Freud in his problematic dealings with punishment dreams and trauma dreams. These types of dreams did not easily fit into the wish fulfillment model and Freud struggled to account for them without making major revisions to his theory. It will be further seen that from these early beginnings there were a number of significant influences arising out of the general body of changing psychoanalytic theory that fostered new and evolving views of the dream. These influences, however, did not engender revised models of dream function and formation. In this exploration it will become clearer that in order to use the manifest content as a meaningful communication, there is the necessity of postulating a process within the psyche that is creating and expressing such a communication.

Deviations in Method Beginning With Freud

In considering Freud's dream theory as it evolved from its beginning in 1900 to its last substantive revision in 1933, two inconsistencies become apparent: his theoretically unsupported use of manifest content in dealing with certain types of symbols and his inability to adequately explain trauma and punishment dreams. These inconsistencies, it is proposed, reveal problems in the basic understanding of dream formation and Freud's neglect of these problems resulted in the gradual disconnect between dream theory and psychoanalytic theory.

Freud tended to ignore controversial innovations such as the work of Ferenczi (1922), Stekel, (1938), and Fairbairn, (1931). In each of these cases, innovations in dream theory were advanced in relation to the general fabric of psychoanalytic theory. Ferenczi (1922) postulated that the trauma dream,

Frank Faranda

a noted problem in the wish-fulfillment model, was an attempt by the ego to repair psychic damage. Also ignored by Freud was the work of Fairbairn (1931) who notes a series of dreams in a long analysis that he was unable to fit into the wish-fulfillment model. Fairbairn formed an idea of dreams as representations of the inner world of the patient. Stekel (1938), also an innovator in dream theory, proposed a dramatic shift in the technique of dream analysis by disputing the basic formulation of radical associationalism. Stekel held that the associations to the manifest content could actually lead the analyst astray. Instead, he opted for an 'intuitive method' where the manifest content is interpreted as a meaningful representation of psychic experience.

Freud's Use of the Manifest

Several anomalies within TIOD are identified by Lansky (1992). He notes that the dreams in TIOD are Freud's own, and that they are not analyzed following the methods proposed in Freud's model.

> The celebrated 'specimen dream' put forward in chapter 2, for example, is analyzed only to the point of demonstrating that the associative method leads to Freud's preconscious preoccupation concerning the circumstances of Irma's mishandled treatment and especially with exculpating himself in the eyes of his colleagues in the face of charges of incompetence. (Lansky, 1992, p. 5)

Lansky goes on to note that through this method, the deepest unconscious impulses, the postulated infantile material that is the source of the dream, is not revealed. Freud's associational method, where the dreamer associates to the elements in the manifest content as a way to reach the unconscious, is not followed. Rather, Lansky states, Freud only takes his dreams to the level of day-residue, the conscious concerns of his waking life. Much of the analysis in TIOD centers, not on Freud's infantile conflicts, but on issues of status and competition.

From the very beginning, however, Freud was absolutely clear in his writings about the basic notion of latent and manifest dream thoughts: the meaning of a dream comes from the latent dream thoughts and not the manifest dream. Lansky (1992) sums up this process as follows

> The manifest dream was the result of transformation of the latent content through the operation of dream work. It was the latent content,

like the repressed memory in psychoneuroses, that was in continuity with the mainstream of mental life and it is this continuity that is the object, not only of dream analysis, but of psychoanalysis. (p. 11)

Lansky (1992) goes on to link Freud's approach to the manifest content to an idea of suspicion

The view of the nature of conflict and defense led Freud to a radical distrust of the manifest content, which in a famous metaphor, he likened to the façade of an Italian church, the appearance of which gave no real sense of what was behind it...the Model held Freud captive, so much so that he put forward the notion of manifest and latent content somewhat inconsistently. (p. 12)

This inconsistency extends to the ironic fact that although in theory Freud, forbade the use of the manifest dream, in actuality, he used it quite freely. As Lansky (1992) states

There is widespread agreement that the manifesto put forward in chapter 2 and alluded to elsewhere is overstated...Freud actually used the manifest content of dreams in a number of different ways, especially symbols, typical dreams, and traumatic dreams. (p.12)

Saul (1958) furthers this notion

Freud's dream of the Botanical monograph did deal with his writing a book and with his botanical discoveries, even though the details could not have been deduced from the manifest dream alone...his dream of digging in a grave dealt with defenses against anxiety about death. His dream of sitting at a dinner table having a lovely lady admire his eyes expressed, as his association and interpretation show, his wishes for love for his own sake and not only as reward for years of hard work and accomplishment. (pp. 129-130)

In speaking of the manifest dream, Freud (1933) states, "You must not suppose that we think nothing of this endless diversity in manifest dreams. We shall come back to it later and we shall find a great deal in it that we can make use of in our interpretations" (p. 35). One of the main ways that

Freud tended toward a use of the manifest was in his approach to symbols. The presence of symbols in dreams was an instance when Freud allowed for an interpretation of the manifest level without associations.

From his comments on the subject of symbols there appear to be two very different ways he makes use of them. The first is what most clinicians would consider 'symbolic interpretation.' An example of this would be interpreting the meaning of bags to represent women's sex organs and staircases to represent the male sex organ (1900). There is a second way that Freud (1933) notes. The example he cites comes from Silberer (1909) who states, "I saw myself planning a piece of wood." Freud notes that this dream came to Silberer when he dozed off while rewriting a passage in an essay. This second way of considering the symbol is very closely related to a commonsense understanding of the dream that any clinician today would have little difficulty appreciating. This use of the manifest symbol is a figurative usage which yields a meaning without associations. Silberer refers to this type of representation as functional. It is not at all clear why Freud allows this instance of manifest interpretation to be valid without adherence to his method. Freud (1933) displays these two types of symbolic material in dreams by noting that a bridge can be a symbol for the male sex organ or it can be a symbol for any idea that acts as a bridge from one element to another. Again, the later use represents an experience-near approach that is familiar and understandable, but exists without an accompanying theory to support its basis for meaning.

The Two Problem Areas

In 1933 Freud made his final revisions to the theory of dreams. As an entrée to his discussion, Freud asks whether all dreams can be interpreted using the model of wish fulfillment. He states, "the answer is: no not all, but so many that we feel confident in the serviceability and correctness of the procedure" (p. 37). In speculating on why there are exceptions, Freud states that oftentimes interpretation takes place against resistance and if the patient is too resistant then you can't get to the associations that would lead to the latent meaning. As always, Freud offers a brilliant solution. But beyond the scope of resistance, Freud speaks of two types of dreams that he acknowledges as authentic exceptions to the rule: punishment dreams and trauma dreams.

Punishment dreams, dreams where harsh and painful scenarios are enacted and negative affect is generated in the dreamer, were always difficult to explain using the wish fulfillment model. Initially, Freud (1900) did not include these dreams. Discussion of the punishment dream was added as addenda to TIOD in the 1911, 1919 and 1930 editions. Freud also dealt with these dreams in <u>Remarks on the Theory and Practice of Dream Interpretation</u> (1923b).

In 1911 Freud relates punishment dreams to masochistic tendencies. Later however, in 1919 and 1923, he contradicts this earlier view by stating that punishment dreams are not to be attributed to a repressed, instinctual wish, i.e. to masochism, but rather to the operation of the self-critical agency of the ego. In the 1930 edition of TIOD, he refers to this agency by the term currently familiar to us, the super-ego.

Weiss (1986) states that these dreams are so unpleasant that "how then can they be regarded as fulfillment of an infantile libidinal wish" (p. 215). Weiss goes on to say that Freud (1919) solved this problem by stating that the punishment dream is a wish for punishment for having the forbidden wish. Freud (1933) expresses this as

> Punishment dreams, too, are fulfillment of wishes, though not of wishes of instinctual impulses but of those of the critical, censoring, and punishing agency of the mind. (p. xx)

Lorand (1956) quotes Alexander as saying "not a single example [of a punishment dream] can be found in Freud's work or in any other publication" (p. 124). This absence of examples is uncharacteristic of Freud and thus noteworthy.

Posing a greater problem for Freud was the trauma dream. His views on these types of dreams also changed through the course of his work. By 1933 Freud held that there were only two serious problems for the wish fulfillment model: adult trauma dreams and childhood trauma dreams. He states (1933) of the former "what wishful impulse could be satisfied by harking back in this way to this exceedingly distressing traumatic experience? It is hard to guess" (p.50).

Freud (1920) expresses the idea that these dreams are endeavoring to master the situation by developing anxiety that was lacking at the time of the trauma. He states that these dreams "afford us a view of a function of the mental apparatus which, though it does not contradict the pleasure principle, is nevertheless independent of it and seems to be more primitive than the purpose of gaining pleasure and avoiding unpleasure" (p. 32).

By 1933 Freud was still working to understand the nature of childhood trauma dreams.

> We can understand their [the painful experience of childhood] having being repressed; but, that being so, we cannot understand how it is that they have such free access to dream life, that they provide the pattern for so many dream-phantasies and that dreams are filled with reproductions of these scenes from childhood and with allusions to them. (1933, p. 50)

Freud wonders if, because these painful experiences are closely linked to infantile sexuality, they become linked to the wishes of the infantile psyche from which the dream emerges, as if the traumatic memories come along for the ride. But what isn't made explicit is why the censor, so important in the formation of the manifest dream, would allow these experiences to bypass the defenses and so disturb sleep. In other words, why are they left undisguised?

Freud (1933), in his final revision to dream theory, and perhaps in response to these issues, offers a significant emendation to his wish fulfillment model.

> We say that a dream is a fulfillment of a wish; but if you want to take these later objections into account, you can say that a dream is an *attempt* at the fulfillment of a wish. No one who can properly appreciate the dynamics of the mind will suppose that you have said anything different by this. In certain circumstance a dream is only able to put its intention into effect very incompletely, or must abandon it entirely. Unconscious fixation to a trauma seems to be foremost among the obstacles to the function of dreaming. (p. 50-51)

What Freud does not allow to enter into his conceptualization is the possibility that trauma dreams are not only unruly exceptions or failed attempts at disguise, but rather, clear representatives of a functional and formational model that is attempting to fulfill a purpose other than the maintenance of equilibrium and the preservation of sleep. In the language of this essay, this other purpose could be understood as the healing function of the Purposive Self.

Influences in the Shift Toward the Use of the Manifest Dream

Current use of the dream in treatment has lessened in importance (Lippmann, 2000) and simultaneously shifted from a clear theoretical approach, as in Freud's original wish fulfillment model, to a theoretically unsupported and vague approach (Fosshage, 2000) that values the manifest dream. It has been established that these two phenomena are interrelated. It has also been established that the movement to the manifest dream would have required a theory capable of explaining the production of a meaningful communication emerging from the unconscious and reaching consciousness through the symbolic experience of dreaming. What remains to be understood are the specific ways in which this shift took shape. By examining these specific influences, it will be possible to better understand the nature of the mechanisms that have been underrepresented in the theory of dreams.

The major influences in the history of psychoanalysis that have impacted the interpretation of dreams are focused in three different areas. The first is related to a changing view of the inner world of the patient, the second is related to technical demands of treatment, and the third is related to a changing view of the unconscious. In broadest terms, these ideas entered the field of psychoanalysis in a chronological progression—first there occurred a shift in the view of the inner world of the patient, next there were major changes in technique, and finally there was a change in the view of the unconscious. In point of fact, however, these shifts formed threads that continued to develop throughout the history of psychoanalysis and influenced dream interpretation and psychoanalytic theory in an ongoing manner.

Imperatives of Technique

Klein's Child Analysis

In 1932 Klein published <u>The Psycho-analysis of Children</u> and extended Freud's model to include the treatment of children. In addition to this specific contribution to the field of psychoanalysis, Melanie Klein's work constituted the formal beginnings of Object Relations theory (Ogden, 1986). As important as these contributions were to the general field, there was a secondary influence of her work that has gone unacknowledged. This contribution relates to the present inquiry in terms of a link between the play of children and the dream of the adult; Klein (1932) both explicitly and implicitly draws a parallel between the two psychic productions. She states (1932)

> If we wish to understand the child's play correctly in relation to its whole behavior during the analytic session we must not be content to pick out the meaning of the separate symbols in the play, striking as they often are, but must take into consideration all the mechanisms and methods of representation employed in the *dream-work*, never losing sight of the relation of each factor to the situation as a whole...all these things are seen to have method in them and will become meaningful if we interpret them as we do dreams. (p. 8; italics mine)

Klein states that play must be interpreted in the same manner as dreams. What this would mean in 1932 would be that the analyst would get associations to the individual elements and ignore the manifest dream story. In support of this she states, "If we make use of this play technique we soon find that the child brings as many associations to the separate elements of its play as adults do to the separate elements of their dreams" (p. 8). Later, however she clarifies her view by linking the elements of play to the associations themselves.

> Just as associations to dream-elements lead to the uncovering of the latent content of the dream, so do the elements of children's play, which correspond to those associations, afford a view of its latent content. (ibid, p. 18)

From this statement her meaning begins to become clearer. She states that the "elements of the child's play" correspond to the "associations" to a dream. So it is not that the child associates to the elements in his play, but rather that the elements in his play are the equivalent of associations. This would mean that the play of the child, the figurative story that is enacted, is one step closer to the latent meaning, than is the dream. What this also means is that the play of the child can be interpreted as a meaningful expression of a psychic situation. This, then, does not in actuality represent a direct equivalence between the dream and the play of a child. And further it does not represent an equivalence of interpretive technique.

To further clarify this difference, consider Klein's (1932) comments on the reparative motives in the play of children.

In its play, even the quite small child will attempt to overcome its un-pleasurable experiences as Freud himself demonstrated in the play of a small boy of one and a half [Freud, 1920, p. 14]. The child threw away a wooden reel tied to a piece of string so that it disappeared and then (by pulling it back into sight again) made it reappear. By doing this over and over again, he attempted to master an unpleasant event—the temporary absence of the mother—psychically. Freud has recognized in his behavior a function of general importance in the play of children. Through play the child turns the experience it has passively endured into an active one and changes unpleasure into pleasure by giving its originally unpleasurable experience a happy ending…Early analysis has shown that in play the child not only overcomes painful reality, but at the same time it also uses it to master its instinctual fears and internal dangers by projecting them into the outer world. (p. 177)

From this example, two major ideas reveal themselves. Following the idea that the child's play is an equivalent of the dream, is the idea that in the play, and also in the dream, there is a meaningful representation of a problem; the difficulty of the child who metaphorically struggles with the idea of loss. In relation to the dream, this would imply that the problem would be meta-phorically visible in the manifest content. A second implication is the notion of repair in the play and the possible link of this to an understanding of the dream as reparative.

Michael Fordham, a Jungian analyst in London, highly influenced by Melanie Klein, states (1995) "The first thing to notice is that they [Klein's interventions] are not so much interpretations as translations into a different language" (p. 51). In this, there is support for the conceptualization that is here being developed. Klein does appear to be translating the meaning of the child's play into a different language. If this were applied to the dream, one would translate the manifest dream into a different language. This type of dream analysis is quite different from Freud's model of radical associationalism.

Klein's work with the play of the child not only impacted child analy-sis, but deepened our understanding of symbol formation and the ways in which the psyche was capable of using symbolic material for the growth and development of the individual.

Frank Faranda

Stekel's Concern for Time

Stekel was an early dissenter from Freud and developed ideas that differed from him in many ways. He believed that Freudian psychoanalysis at that point in time, 1938, was rigid and orthodox and that there was a pressure to conduct analysis according to a "table of laws" (Stekel, 1938, p. ix). Stekel believed that psychoanalysis in 1938 was in a crisis. He was concerned that the length of treatment was beginning to grow far too long and that this was a bad sign (Gutheil, 1951). Related to this he states (1938)

> Still, from his (Freud's) books and from what I have been told by his patients, I know that the master analyzed some of his cases for two or three years. In one instance he reports, that of an obsessional disease, the 'basic trauma' was not disclosed until after three years' laborious analysis. (p. x)

Stekel views three years as a long analysis

> It is obvious that so long a treatment must be reserved for the elect, needing as it does immense expenditure of time and money, and perhaps making an excessive demand upon patience as well. For my part, a good many years ago I declared that the best results could be achieved in a comparatively brief time, not exceeding three or four months. (ibid, p. x)

Regardless of the validity of Stekel's concern, his interest in reducing the length of treatment led him to devalue the method of free association. He states, "Additional experience has convinced me that we can make no progress when our attention is confined to the patient's associations" (p. x). He believed that the associations actually led the analyst away from the true problem. There is the further question raised by Stekel as to whether the free associations are actually free at all. He believed, to the contrary, that the analyst was continually influencing the flow (Stekel, 1938; Gutheil, 1951).

Because of these perceived problems, the length of treatment and the uncertainty about free association, Stekel, like Rank and Ferenczi, worked to develop ways to shorten the treatment.

Stekel's school was highly engaged in the use of dreams to shorten the period of analysis. It was their belief that the dream was a quick road to understanding the unconscious material. He states, "Those that belong to my school start from the fact that the patient has a psychical scotoma, that there is something he will not or cannot see. With the aid of dream interpretation, that something can be discovered, the solution to the mental conflict being thus hastened" (p. 232). He adds, "Psychoanalysis without the aid of dreams is only possible if there are actual conflicts. When we are dealing with the experiences of childhood, no progress can be made in default of dream interpretation" (p. 236).

Stekel's model was further developed by Emil Gutheil, a name that has disappeared from the psychoanalytic culture, but one that was important to dream theory for a time. Gutheil was the protégé of Wilhelm Stekel and was director of the Postgraduate Center in New York after he left Nazi Germany. He died in 1959 and published a large book that documents Stekel's theory as it relates to the broad territory of the history of dream interpretation and specifically Freud's model. In Gutheil's book, The Handbook of Dream Analysis, (1951) there is a mix of classical Freudian conceptions and progressive alterations in method. Gutheil elaborates a model of analytical work developed originally by Stekel that was more "active" than the Freudian model from which it emerged. In this way of working, the analyst is not wedded to the free association of the patient, but moves forward using intuition and the accumulated knowledge he has of the patient. Gutheil states that Freud "asks the dreamer to disregard the manifest dream content and turn his attention away from the dream as a whole" (p. 247). He goes on to note the difference in Stekel's method

> The method of interpretation described in this chapter represents, in part, a deviation from the standard technique as it is practiced by Freud and his school. In order to render the analytic method more efficient and to reduce the duration of the average treatment, a reformed technique of interpreting the analytic material has been introduced by Stekel and his school. (p. 248)

The first element in this method of dream interpretation involves a "simplification" of the manifest content that will be clear in the following example.

> To 'simplify' a dream means to reduce its whole content to an outline, to a few words. Let us do this with the following dream of a sixteen year old boy...*I dreamed I was back in high school and lived in the same*

boarding house. I saw my schoolmate Douglas with a pipe in his mouth. I was
surprised at this, for he had never smoked before.
Then I was in Elizabeth's house and all her other boy friends were there too. I
left irritated and jealous—I wanted to have her to myself.
Then I dreamed that I was with my mother and the assistant principle of my
high school. The latter asked me some questions about Canada and I answered
in the negative.

"Conclusions: (1) the dreamer sees himself in the past, in his high
school days. Simplification: return to the past. (2) He is surprised at
seeing his former friend smoking as he has never done this before. Simplification: People have changed. (3) He is then in his friend's house
and feels jealous. Simplification: Rivalry, jealousy, and a desire for possession. (4) He sees the mother with the asst. principle (father figure)
answers negative to questions about Canada. (The dreamer's step father
lives in Canada.) Simplification: Opposition to the parents." (p. 249)

From this Gutheil surmises that the dreamer is experiencing the loss of love
from his mother, jealousy, and the grief that things have changed. He is in
opposition to the parents. These formulations are a use of the manifest dream
as a metaphoric, or figurative representation of the inner conflicts. In this
method, the analyst is not using the associations to lead to the latent dream,
but is attempting to understand the language of the dream as a representation of the problem: a communication in a different language.

It can be surmised that Stekel's ideas may have had an effect on the
psychoanalytic approach to dreams. Specifically, the emphasis on using the
manifest content was very revolutionary at the time and although Stekel and
Gutheil have not remained a part of current theory, one can imagine that
their work trickled into the general approach to working with dreams. As
head of the Post Graduate Center, Gutheil undoubtedly influenced a whole
generation of analysts in their clinical treatment of dreams.

A View of The Inner World

The changing view of the inner world of the unconscious began with
the nascent formulations of Object Relations inherent in Freud's work between 1915 and 1923. During that time, Freud wrote <u>Mourning and Melan-</u>
<u>cholia</u> and <u>The Ego and the Id</u>. These two works constitute the beginning

of a shift in how the inner world of the patient is conceived. In the changing view, object representations and interactions between internal structures replace the topographical ideas of repression and discharge. As will be seen, there is a clear parallel between the view of the inner world and the view of the manifest dream: both being conceived as being populated by aspects of the personality.

Fairbairn's Endopsychic Structures

In 1931 Fairbairn published an account of an analysis of a woman whose dreams and fantasies helped Fairbairn to extend the work of Freud on the nature of dream experience. The woman tended to personify certain aspects of her psychic experience and these figures appeared quite regularly, in varying forms, in the manifest content of her dreams. Originally, Fairbairn conceived of these figures as representations of the ego, id, and super ego. But soon the cast of characters extended beyond the structural model to what came to be known as the Object Relations model.

By 1944 Fairbairn continued to develop the ideas from 1931 on the nature of the dream in relation to the endopsychic situation. Looking back at the 1931 case he states

> Among the dreams recorded by this woman were a number which defied all efforts to bring them into conformity with the 'wish-fulfillment' theory, and which she herself came to describe quite spontaneously as 'state of affairs' dreams, intending by this description to imply that they represented actually existing endopsychic situations. Doubtless this made an impression on me. At any rate, much later, after Freud's theory of psychical structure had become familiar, after Melanie Klein had elaborated the conceptions of psychical reality and internal objects and after I myself had become impressed by the prevalence and importance of schizoid phenomena, I tentatively formulated the view that all figures appearing in dreams represented either parts of the dreamer's own personality (conceived in terms of ego, super-ego and id) or else identifications on the part of the ego. A further development of this view was to the effect that dreams are essentially, not wish-fulfillments, but dramatizations or 'shorts' (in the cinemographic sense) of situations existing in inner reality...according to my present view, therefore, the situations depicted in dreams represent relationships existing between endopsychic structures. (p. 99)

Fairbairn's theory of dreams emerged directly out of his developing clinical theory of object relations (Winnicott, 1953). And by 1944, in the endopsychic paper, Fairbairn was completely wedded to the idea of interpreting the dream on the manifest level. He views the dream in terms of the drama that is being enacted.

Padel (1978) states, "For clinical purposes Fairbairn and others who base their work on his assume that dreams are representations of endopsychic situations over which the dreamer has got stuck (fixation points) and often include some attempt to move beyond that situation" (p. 133). This offers another implication of Fairbairn's view; the dream is not only offering a representation, but also an attempt at repair.

As noted in Chapter Two, Fairbairn did not extend his theories to a complete model of mental functioning. As Winnicott (1953) noted, Fairbairn did not develop a way to account for primary creativity and thus was not able to form a theoretical model for dream production. Rather, he simply changed his clinical technique based on clinical realities without extrapolating back to a reformulation of the model of the mind.

Perls & Gestalt Therapy

Occurring at roughly the same point in the history of psychoanalysis, Fritz Perls emerged with the development of Gestalt therapy. Like Fairbairn, Perls viewed the inner world of the patient as populated by aspects of the personality that possess relative degrees of relationship to the ego. This view of the psyche was founded on the idea that psychic conflicts create oppositions and that an individual is pressured to repudiate certain aspects in order to maintain affiliation, self-esteem, and adherence to desired self-qualities. The unwanted parts of the personality, then, are split off from the main. In Perls' view, it is this split whole that needs to be re-integrated through therapy.

Perls' view of the psyche is reflected in his view of the dream. Like Fairbairn, Perls (1949) holds that the manifest dream illustrates the different aspects of the personality in relationships and conflicts. The function of the dream is a way for the psyche to manage and distance itself from the unwanted parts. The dream is a projection and the goal of dream analysis is the assimilation of these aspects back into the whole of the person. Perls (1949) states

There are at least two types of dreams, pleasant and unpleasant. The pleasant dreams are direct or indirect completions of incomplete situations: they coincide with the wish-fulfillment in Freud's terminology. The unpleasant dreams invariably contain projections, their best known prototype being the nightmare. The person or animal which dominates the nightmare is always an unwanted part of yourself. If you dream you are being bitten by a poisonous snake it might be correct to interpret the snake as an aggressive phallus symbol, but it is more useful to search for the poisonous snake hidden in your own character. Whenever the dental aggression is not expressed, but projected, you will find yourself, in your dreams, chased by dogs, lions and other animals symbolic of biting. Projected wishes to be a burglar, a killer, a policeman or other puerile ideals will appear in the dream, as fear of being assaulted or arrested. (p. 240)

Although it is difficult to know the full impact of Fairbairn and Perls on the methods employed in dream interpretation, it is probable that they had a great deal. More important, however, than the specific trail of influence, is the overall shift within the field of psychoanalysis toward a somewhat personified view of the inner world and the manifest dream. It is the view of this essay that this shift was related to dream interpretation in two ways. This change in the view of the inner world allowed clinicians to observe what was perhaps always present in the dream but unobservable without a template for apperception. In other words, clinicians began to notice that the figurative relationships between the characters in the dream reflected the figurative pattern of the inner world of the dreamer. The other way in which this shift in the field impacted dream interpretation was the inverse of this phenomenon. As the view of the dream began to change, it allowed clinicians to see the inner world of the patient more clearly.

A Changing View of the Unconscious

A second paradigm shift that influenced the interpretation of dreams occurred through the change of value attributed to the unconscious. Implicit in Freud's model was the notion of suspicion and this was explicit in the classical approach to the manifest dream (Lansky 1992). But during the period after WWII, two major figures emerged within the field of psychoanalysis that challenged this view with a more positive regard for the manifestations of the unconscious. These two figures were Karen Horney and Erich Fromm. Interestingly enough, while the use of dreams in analysis was waning for most analysts, both Horney and Fromm developed a rich appreciation for the dream (Gershman, 1981).

Horney's Constructive Forces

Karen Horney developed a model of the mind that included a 'force' that works positively for the greater integration and development of the personality. This basic view was also applied to the dream and dream interpretation.

Gershman, a modern follower of Horney, states that Horney "was able to integrate a system of dream interpretation that incorporated the best contributions of all her predecessors" (p. 221). He states that the difference between Freud and Horney on the use of dreams was that Horney appreciated Freud's concepts but

> Freud believed that the dream must disguise feelings in order to bypass the censor and therefore the manifest content of the dream must be interpreted in such a manner as to disclose what lies beneath the dream, whereas Horney had a different approach. (pp. 221-222)

For Horney, dreams reveal the constructive forces of the psyche more clearly than other psychic material. Gershman (1981) states this viewpoint in relation to Freud

> Unlike Freud, who felt that the dream is a disguised distortion of underlying instinctual wishes, Horney looked upon the dream as a more truthful holistic expression of the patient's current conflicts and as evidence of his mode of coping with them, whether constructively or destructively. The dream is one of the most sensitive instruments for revealing the patient's constructive or destructive solutions to his conflicts. (p. 228)

In these comments are the two interrelated ideas on the question of dream interpretation. The first is that the unconscious is viewed with a positive regard and attributed a purposiveness and the second is that the manifest dream is viewed without suspicion, as an attempt to communicate and integrate.

Fromm's Trust in the Rational Unconscious

Erich Fromm developed a way of working with dreams that directly used the manifest dream as a meaningful communication. This use, as with Horney, was intimately related to his view of the unconscious. Fromm made explicit his ideas on the dream in his book, The Forgotten Language, (1951). In this work, Fromm acknowledges the contributions of Jung and also identified the ways in which he differs from both Freud and Jung.

> My definition of dreaming as any kind of mental activity under the condition of sleep, while based upon Freud's theory of dreams, is in sharp contrast to it in many ways. My assumption is that dreams can be the expression both of the lowest and most irrational and of the highest and most valuable functions of our minds. (p. 47)

He notes that Freud had a view of the dream as exclusively representative of the irrational in man, the infantile id speaking out. Fromm, however, had a different understanding of the unconscious that is likewise reflected in his view of the dream. Fromm (1951) quotes Jung as saying, "that the unconscious mind is capable at times of assuming an intelligence and purposiveness which are superior to actual conscious insight" (Jung, 1948, p. 45). Fromm amends this by stating, "Thus far I have no quarrel with this statement and it corresponds to my own experience with dream interpretation outlined above" (p. 96). But Fromm then departs from Jung

> The difference between Jung's interpretation and my own can be summed up in this statement. There is agreement that we often are wiser and more decent in our sleep than in our waking life. Jung explains this phenomenon with the assumption of a source of revelation transcending us, while I believe that what we think in our sleep is *our* thinking, and that there are good reasons for the fact that the influences we are submitted to in our waking life have in many respects a stultifying effect on our intellectual and moral accomplishment. (1951, p. 97)

But regardless of this difference, the important ideas that relate to the interpretation of manifest content are clearly evident. Fromm (1951) holds that the unconscious is decent and rational and that the dream, as a product of the unconscious, is a representation of these factors. Also, this view of the unconscious and the dream allows Fromm to believe that the manifest dream is not a disguise or a deception but an authentic communication.

Conclusion: What Must the Mind Be Like?

Freud's model of dream theory was perfect in form and seamlessly interwoven with his theory of the mind. The instinctual infantile sexual wish was an energy that threatened to disturb sleep and the dreamwork transformed the energy of this wish into the disguised dream that evaded the censor and preserved sleep. In much the same way, the neurotic symptom was a transformation of an unacceptable impulse.

In Freud's model, several difficult questions related to the dream were answered: where does the dream come from?; why does it come forth?; what propels the dream?; and what determines the form the dream takes? And for the most part, Freud's model stood the test of clinical application. For when viewed from within the framework of Freud's general theory and metapsychology, his understanding of the dream follows a logical line.

As noted, however, certain types of dreams clearly defied interpretation using the wish fulfillment model and instead of Freud rethinking the nature of the dream, he simply noted that there were exceptions to the rule. Trauma dreams were the most salient examples of these exceptions, but other variations emerged which began to open the possibility for understanding the dream as something other than a disguise.

Over time, clinicians began to make adjustments to the rule of radical associationalism that was the bedrock of Freud's model. Changes in the general theory of psychoanalysis, the understanding of the inner world, changes in technique, and the changing view of the unconscious, all contributed to a clinical recognition that the dream as a manifest expression had meaning to the dreamer, to his inner world, and to the process of treatment.

It is here that one discerns a separation of dream interpretation from dream theory. The result is a clinical technique that has no support from the underlying model of the mind, model of development, or model of psychopathology. Freud's original vision for an integrated theory able to account both for the dream and the neurotic symptom is lost. From the perspective of this essay, the reason no theory developed to account for the dream is due to the implications of such a theory; it requires a concept of inherent purpose within the psyche.

Chapter Four: Background on Jung and the Link to the Purposive Self

This chapter will begin to build a theoretical model that is capable of supporting an understanding of the Purposive Self and the dream as a manifestation of that purposivity. Jungian theory, although relatively unacknowledged in the psychoanalytic dialogue, offers the potential for building such a model through integration with contemporary clinical theories of the self.

Before proceeding to offer specifics from Jungian theory on the Self and the dream, this chapter will explore the parallel between the absence of Jung from the psychoanalytic discussion and the absence of theoretical ideas on the self as purposive from psychoanalytic theory. This exploration will begin with a look at the highly charged relationship of Freud and Jung and extend outward to include theory, culture, and philosophy.

History & Background

In 1900, the year Freud published <u>The Interpretation of Dreams</u>, Jung began his work at the Burgholzi Mental Hospital in Zurich. At that time, Burgholzi was one of the finest institutions for the care of severely ill psychiatric patients. This population included hysterics and obsessional neurotics, but also, more important to Jung's development, Dementia Praecox (schizophrenic) patients.

In 1903 Jung married Emma Rauschenbach, the daughter of a wealthy businessman. The newlyweds moved into a flat in the main building of the Burgholzi Hospital and lived there for 5 years.

The beginning of the Freud/Jung connection began in 1901 when, at the request of Eugene Bleuler, the head of Burgholzi, Jung prepared a review of Freud's <u>On Dreams</u>, which Jung then presented to the staff doctors at the hospital. The impact of Freud's work on Jung can be inferred from the fact that in 1902 when Jung published his medical dissertation he mentioned Freud four times. As F.X. Charet (1993), a lecturer in psychology and religion states, "it is evident [from Jung's 1907 foreword to <u>The Psychology of</u>

Dementia Praecox] that Jung was aware of Freud's theory of sexuality..." (p. 174). Later, in 1906, Jung publicly defended Freud from the attacks of a leading pundit Gustav Aschaffenburg at a conference in Baden-Baden. Freud was not in attendance.

Meanwhile, Freud had heard of Jung and already purchased his 1906 Diagnostic Association Studies by the time Jung had sent him a copy as a form of introduction. Thus began the lengthy correspondence between the two men, a correspondence that would last from April 1, 1906 to January 6, 1913 when Jung agreed to Freud's request to end their personal relations. Jung closed the final letter with the words from Hamlet, "the rest is silence." During the years of their correspondence, 344 letters were exchanged.

The initial meeting between the two men took place in March of 1907 when Jung visited Freud in Vienna. The first day together they talked for thirteen hours without interruption. In 1908, at the insistence of Freud, Jung became the editor of the first journal of psychoanalysis known as "the yearbook". That year Freud visited Jung and stayed in the Jung's flat at Burgholzi. By February of 1909, the first yearbook came out and later that year each of them, Freud and Jung, were invited to Clark University in Massachusetts to lecture on psychoanalysis. In attendance at this conference were, among others, Jones, Ferenczi, Freud and Jung from Europe and William James and James Jackson Putnam from America. In 1910 Jung was made the first president of the International Psychoanalytic Association and also published the first volume of his controversial The Psychology of the Unconscious which contained views in contrast to those of Freud (Abraham, 1914). These views concerned the role of sexuality in neuroses, the nature of libido, and the centrality of the Oedipal complex. In simplified form, the contrast of Jung's early views to those of Freud could be said to hinge on Jung's relativization of sexuality in understanding psychological dynamics. In 1912 the separation grew more complete when Jung was invited again to America to deliver a series of lectures on psychoanalysis at Fordham University. Freud was not in attendance thus granting Jung carte blanche in presenting his views as they differed from Freud.

In November of 1912 Freud had his fainting fit in Munich at a psychoanalytic conference. This fit was the second fainting episode Freud had in Jung's presence. At this second episode Jung picked Freud up from the ground and carried him to a nearby couch. As he did so, Freud looked up at Jung and said, "how sweet it must be to die." Freud interpreted these faints in various ways to various individuals. His representation of the meaning ranged from being over worked to an unconscious acknowledgement of Jung's death wish for Freud. The context for each of these faints was a discussion of archeology. In the first, it was a talk of buried mummies discovered in Germany, and the second was related to the removal of the father's name from palace walls in ancient Egypt after the son of a dead ruler took over the throne.

Two months after the last faint, the correspondence between Freud and Jung ended. Six months after that Jung resigned as editor of the journal and within a year Jung resigned as president of the International Psychoanalytic Association. The rest was silence.

In reading the Freud/Jung letters (McGuire, 1974), one is immediately aware of how powerfully these two men connected. It is also equally apparent how painfully they split apart. After the friendship failed, Freud vilified Jung in print, never mentioned his accomplishments, and never again allowed any man into his intimate association (Jones, 1955). For Jung, the years after the split were a time of fragmentation and isolation. Jung abandoned all responsibilities and positions and did not write for three years. What isn't clear, however, is why these two very different men came together in the first place, what made their connection so powerful and why they failed to maintain this alliance?

Early in 1895, just after enrolling in medical school Jung became a member of the Zofingia Society, a student fraternity at Basel University. During his time with the Society, he delivered five lectures oriented toward philosophy, spirituality, and the occult. A review of these lectures reveals early signs that Jung's concept for a purposive unconscious was already present in nascent form before meeting Freud. William McGuire, the editor of the published lectures states, "these lectures...anticipate his [Jung's] mature interest in empirical psychology, spiritualism, the occult, and the metaphysical" (p. xiv).

In Charet's (1993) view, Jung was from the very beginning of his career focused on the spiritual and the religious. But, Charet states, "his interest in these [spiritualistic] phenomena was purely psychological" (p. 172). In 1905, well into his career as a psychiatrist yet before meeting Freud, Jung gave a lecture "On Spiritualistic Phenomena" at Basel University. In this lecture Jung remarked on the dual nature of his interest in these phenomena

> The dual nature of spiritualism…on the one side a religious sect, on the other a scientific hypothesis—spiritualism touches upon widely differing areas of life that would seem to have nothing in common. (p. 293)

Charet, in speaking of the early influences on Jung states that Jung was influenced by Theodore Flournoy and Pierre Janet "both of whom investigated spiritualistic phenomena" (p. 172). That these interests of Jung's were central to his thinking is to be seen by a brief look at Jung's Medical dissertation on the psychology of mediumship. Following the work of Flournoy who researched the psychological processes underlying their experience of mediums, Jung undertook to write a dissertation based on his attendance at séances with his cousin Helly Preiswerk. Jung's basic conclusion in his dissertation was that Helly, as a medium, was giving voice to dissociated aspects of her personality. These interests continued throughout his career as evidenced in the 1908 letter Jung wrote to Freud regarding a similar case. Jung states

> Naturally everything fits in with your theory…The early sexual history is not yet clear, since the thirteenth year everything is shrouded in retrograde amnesia. The twilight states are similar to those I first published ("occult Phenomena"). The patient plays to perfection and with positively thrilling dramatic beauty the personality that is her dream ideal. (in McGuire (1974), pp. 107-108)

In this case Jung shows the two sides of his interest, the occult and the psychological. Jung goes on to discuss the treatment using Freud's method of dream interpretation leading to the sexual complex. During this same year, only one year after they met for the first time, Freud began to voice his acknowledgment of Jung's spiritual inclinations. These acknowledgements were seconded by Abraham in a 1908 letter to Freud written while Abraham was in training with Jung at Burgholzi. He states

> I do not wish to worry you with details. But the sudden fading out of the Freudian evenings, so well attended until April, is striking. Jung seems to be reverting to his former spiritualistic inclinations. But please keep this between ourselves. (Abraham & Freud, 1965 p. 43)

Charet (1993) tells us that Freud preferred to believe that Jung's spiritualistic inclinations were an influence of Bleuler, Jung's chief at Burgholzi. Earlier, however, Freud wrote to Jung regarding a difference of opinion on the question of religion stating

> I knew that our views would soon be reconciled, that you had not as I feared, become alienated from me by some inner development deriving from the relationship with your father and the beliefs of the church. (pp. 157-158)

As the earliest work of Jung makes clear, he was from the very start of his career interested in a psychological understanding of the spiritual mysteries of the human condition. As is also clear from the letters of Freud, Jung, and Abraham, Freud was aware from the earliest days that Jung had these interests and did not seem to be leaving them behind with his childhood toys. As Charet (2000) states

> Try as he might Freud could not wean Jung from such spiritual preoccupations and his worst fears were realized when Jung, his appointed heir, began to insinuate them into the theory and practice of psychoanalysis. (p. 196)

As Jung (1963) reports in his autobiography

> Freud said to me, "My dear Jung, promise to never abandon the sexual theory. That is the most essential thing of all. You see, we must make a dogma out of it, an unshakeable bulwark..." I asked him "a bulwark, against what?" To which he replied, "Against the black tide of mud"— and here he hesitated for a moment, then added, "of occultism". (p. 150)

The historian Henri F. Ellenberger in his definitive work <u>The Discovery of the Unconscious</u> (1970) offers a unique perspective on Freud, Jung, and their relationship. Through contextualizing the developments that emerged at the turn of the century into the larger historical fabric of dynamic psychotherapy beginning long before Freud and Jung, Ellenberger is able to bring out underlying cultural, philosophical, and theoretical dimensions that worked to make up the changing world of psychotherapeutic treatment in the hands of Freud and Jung.

In discussing what influenced Jung's ideas, Ellenberger notes several non-positivist scholars such as Janet as being central. From Janet, Jung learned psychological automatism, dual personality, psychological strength and weakness, the function of synthesis, abaisment du niveau mental, and subconscious fixed ideas which Jung later linked to Ziehen's "complexes" and Freud's "traumatic reminiscences" (p. 727). Flournoy, according to Ellenberger, was a major influence; in him Jung found a parallel to his own interest in the occult.

Ellenberger also states that a parallel exists between Jung's later work on extraversion and introversion and the work of Binet on two types of intelligence. However, this link is speculative since no mention of Binet occurs in any of Jung's work on the subject or in any correspondence. Influences on Jung's mythological formulations, Ellenberger believes, stem from Friedrich Creuzer, a German romantic scholar who believed that through the Eleusinian mysteries and ancient myths, priests transmitted wisdom to the initiates. It is believed that Goethe was likewise influenced by Creuzer's study of myth. From Creuzer Jung discovered a "rich mine of myths and symbols with their interpretations" (p. 729).

Ellenberger also believes that Jung was influenced by Bachofen, although Jung rarely quotes him. Bachofen taught methods of interpreting symbols. Another influence Ellenberger finds was from the ethnologist Adolf Bastian who devised a theory of "elementary thoughts." In this theory, Bastian believed that diffusion could not alone explain the occurrence of similar myths and practices all over the world. There must be, according to Bastian, some "universal structure of the human mind" (in Ellenberger, 1970, p. 730). This Ellenberger believes, relates to Jung's later thinking on the collective unconscious.

Reflections on Freud and Jung

Leonard Shengold, a classical analyst, in his critique of The Freud/Jung Letters (1976), offers a view of the relationship from a classical Oedipal vantage point. According to Shengold, the reason for the rupture was due to Jung's inability to "master his conflict about parental authority" (p.681). Shengold tells us that Freud was only culpable in his unwillingness to acknowledge Jung's problem. Shengold goes on to state that Jung attempted to "defend against these feelings by abstraction—in his writings [Jung] treats incest as symbolic; he defends against the current situation in relation to Freud by displacing to the past—he begins to study mythology" (p. 681). He states summarily

> These letters are a record of the relationship of two men of genius that is as fascinating and dramatic as any great novel. Their scientific split was predetermined by the vicissitudes of their Oedipal conflicts. Jung could not master his; Freud struggled in relation to Jung, as he had with Fleiss, to consolidate the most difficult of all insights. He was continuing his "interminable self-analysis", a process he [described as]...an exploration of an "intellectual hell"—a hell in which his parents and himself were frozen at the center. Freud discovered that he was Mephistopheles as well as Faust. The devils were not without but within. For Jung, however, Freud had become an externalized black devil. And in Jung's struggle to achieve exorcism, Freud's insight—the fruit of the "tree of paradise"—was also cast out. (p. 683)

Hans Loewald, reviewed the Freud/Jung correspondence in 1977 for the Psychoanalytic Quarterly. His critique offers a more balanced perspective than Shengold in that Loewald recognizes the mutual influence involved in the Freud/Jung relationship. He states

> Both had been conscious of the intensity and, in some respects, intimacy of their friendship, of the emotional and intellectual demands they made on each other—demands that in the long run neither of them could tolerate, so that the passionate mutual rejection became inevitable. (p. 515)

Loewald comments on the relationship by saying that it "foundered on the rock of the 'father complex'" (p.516). He goes on to say that Freud tried to see in Jung the son and heir while Jung never saw himself that way. Loewald then, I believe, correctly states that Jung did perhaps want a father but not the kind of father that Freud was able to be. He sums up the Freud/Jung relationship and correspondence

Two dedicated men, endowed with exceptional gifts, devoting their lives to the understanding of the unconscious, to the higher development of the mind and of their own and their patients' and students' emotional-intellectual life, came to a love-hate impasse which they could not resolve other than by complete and final disruption of their friendship. (p. 519)

Offering a slightly different perspective in his critique, John Gedo (1983) in his book, Portraits of the Artist examines the Freud/Jung relationship on the basis of failed idealization and creativity. One, Freud's growing dissatisfaction with and inevitable rupture from Jung was due to Jung's reluctance to fully embrace the libido theory; two, that Freud was not emotionally involved with Jung as he was earlier with Fleiss; and three, that Jung had "become an essential figure in Freud's psychological world" (p. 236). Gedo (1983) then makes his thesis regarding the rupture clear when he states, "the roots of the problem must be sought in the mutually contradictory personal requirements that the two men brought to their encounter" (p. 236).

In discussing the dynamics underlying the Freud/Jung relationship, Peter Homans, Professor of Religion and Psychological Studies at the University of Chicago in his book Jung in Context (1979) states that it is "not enough to view it in terms of a regressive father transference: rivalry with the father" (p. 37). He states, "the Freud Jung relationship was a transference, but it was a narcissistic transference" (p. 37). In this model, archaic self-object needs would predominate. Grandiosity and idealization would be followed by devaluation and disappointment. Homans adds that Freud accounted for the separation of the two men by applying his own theory: Jung was acting out his "father complex." The letters contain, according to Homans, Jung's conviction that Freud was becoming increasingly dogmatic and authoritarian about his sexual theory. Homans fairly states that "both men viewed the relationship as a kind of transference, each assigning blame to the other" (p. 48). Homans argues

The Freud-Jung relationship was not simply—perhaps from Jung's point of view, not at all—an oedipal conflict, in which over-intense rivalry exists between a father figure and a son figure. Instead, drawing upon Kohut for theory, and upon his colleague Gedo for application at specific points, I propose that the relationship between the two men was a narcissistic transference and that it underwent a number of vicissitudes that characterize this type of relationship. (p. 49)

Ellenberger (1970) states "there is a basic similarity between the system of Freud and Jung, each one deriving from a creative illness channeled into a psychotherapeutic method. Both offer a journey into the unconscious, but it is a very different journey" (p. 736). And further

> Those who undertake a Freudian analysis will soon develop an intensive transference neurosis, have Freudian dreams, and discover their Oedipus complex, child sexuality, and castration anxiety. Those who undertake a Jungian analysis will have Jungian dreams, confront their shadow, their anima, their archetypes, and pursue their individuation. A Freudian psychoanalyst who would undergo a Jungian analysis would feel as disoriented as Mephisto in the second part of Faust, when he comes to the classical Walpurgis Night and discovers to his amazement that 'there is another hell with its own laws'. (p. 737)

Ellenberger understands the Freud/Jung relationship as important in the development of Jung's ideas, but not as the only influence upon Jung. Jung's "system" of psychology emerged, not from Freud, but from his own explorations in the unconscious in parallel to Freud. Ellenberger states further, however, that Jung never fully accepted Freud's sexual or Oedipal theories, but was a staunch supporter of Freud and psychoanalysis during their collaborative period. In 1909, Ellenberger tells us, Jung expressed the seeds of the separation by stating, "libido is what psychiatrists call will and striving" (p. 695).

Ellenberger goes on to sum up the difference between Jung and Freud by initially noting that Freud's work "is heir to positivism, scientism, and Darwinism, whereas Jung's psychology rejects that heritage and returns to the unaltered sources of psychiatric Romanticism and philosophy of nature" (p. 657).

Given the uniqueness and transparency of their theoretical agendas it leads one to suspect, following Michael Palmer, Academic Tutor in the School of Theology at Westminster College, Oxford as he states in his work Freud and Jung on Religion (1997) that practical issues such as the advancement of Freud's ideas, and increased personal fame and notoriety were involved in bringing and keeping these two men together. Palmer (1997) states

> As Freud often said, Jung was Joshua to his Moses. And from the first Freud was quick to see the practical advantages of this relationship. Not only had Jung proved himself a formidable champion of Freud's theories, not only had his own researches at Burgholzi independently supported them at a time when Freud was still generally reviled within the academic community, but the fact that Jung was not Jewish and not Austrian meant that psychoanalysis could more easily defend itself against charges of intellectual and sectarian elitism and so enlist the sympathetic interest of a much wider audience. (p. 89)

As Jones (1955) reports, "Freud himself perceived the advantage of establishing a broader basis for the work than could be provided by the Viennese Jewry, and so determined that Jung should be appointed the first president of the Psychoanalytic Association" (p. 77). Freud wrote similarly in 1914 by stating

> I felt the need of transferring my authority to a younger man, who would then, as a matter of course take my place after my death. This man could only be C.G. Jung...in favor of Jung were his exceptional talents, the contributions he had already made to psychoanalysis, his independent position, and the impression of energy and assurance which his personality conveyed. (p. 329)

Many commentators echo this view: Jung was needed to bring psychoanalysis to the world. Ellenberger (1970) has stated that without Jung psychoanalysis would not have emerged on the world scene when it did. Loewald also acknowledges that the world-wide emergence of psychoanalysis during the years of 1907-1913 was, in great measure, due to Jung's influence. Loewald states, "this could hardly have been accomplished at that time by the diffident Freud and his Viennese followers alone" (p. 515). And Ronald Hayman (2001) in his new biography <u>A Life of Jung</u> states

> The friendship was to last about seven years—longer than it would have if the mutual need had been merely personal. Both benefited

professionally: the alliance helped to propagate Freud's ideas, while the ideas helped both of them to international fame. (p. 96)

From the above it is clear that professional ambition was important in bringing Freud and Jung together and in making it possible for each of them to overlook differences in the name of progress. Gedo (1983) amplifies this by adding the notion of idealizing transference. Freud repeatedly states that he is not worthy of veneration and instructs Jung to not project religious idealizations onto him. Gedo is correct when he states that "a contemporary reader of the correspondence cannot quite agree that Freud presented himself to Jung as a person unfit for idealization" (p. 243). One cannot help but feel that Freud in his protestations is simply playing the role of the humble leader and that indeed Freud "doth protest too much." Gedo states further, "It is hardly surprising that Jung's propensity for idealization found a suitable object in Freud" (P. 244). Quoting from Jung's autobiography, Gedo writes, "My whole being was seeking for something still unknown which might confer meaning on the banality of life" (Jung 1963, p. 165). Gedo believes that this betrays Jung's need to have Freud be more that just a person with limitations. He states, "Hence he [Jung] became scornful of Freud's viewpoint that, except for the various 'all too human' limitations, nothing much is to be found in Man" (p. 255). This position of Gedo's can be summed up in his statement, "Jung's feeling of injury came through the disappointment of his desperate need to idealize Freud as the prophet of a new therapeutic cult," (p. 257), and in saying that Jung was never able to "maintain a realistic view of Freud. Unless he could attribute magical powers to him he tended to view Freud as a reincarnation of his inadequate father" (p. 259). Gedo, however, believes that the idealization was not part of the father transference, but was a vigorous defense against it (p. 259). Gedo then asserts, "When nobody was available to contain Jung's grandiosity in this manner, he began to feel that his own unconscious was divine" (p. 262). In this statement Gedo gives voice to several aspects of criticism of Jung and Jungian theory. One, Jung was attempting to create a religion. Two, he was deluded in his theoretical formulations by grandiosity. Three, Jung believed that God existed inside him and that this belief rendered his theory un-psychological. Without doubt, these criticisms deserve contemplation. In the interest of opening this area for deeper understanding, I would like to take a slight detour to hear from Jung himself

Frank Faranda

on the issue of God. In 1912, Jung stated in <u>The Psychology of the Unconscious</u>

> The idea of God is an absolutely necessary psychological function of an irrational nature, which has nothing what ever to do with the question of God's existence. The human intellect can never answer this question, still less give any proof of God. Moreover such proof is superfluous, for the idea of an all-powerful divine Being is present everywhere, unconsciously if not consciously...(p. 110)

And in one of his last works <u>Answer to Job</u> (1952) he states

> I have been asked so often whether I believe in the existence of God that I am somewhat concerned lest I be taken for an adherent of "psychologism" far more commonly than I suspect. What most people overlook or seem unable to understand is the fact that I regard the psyche as real. They believe in physical facts, and must consequently come to the conclusion that either the uranium or the laboratory created the atom bomb. That is no less absurd than the assumption that a nonreal psyche is responsible for it. God is an obvious and non-physical fact, i.e., a fact that can be established psychically but not physically. (p. 751)

In these statements Jung focuses on the experiential dimensions of God and religion and attempts to understand this experience as psychological.

Loewald (1977), like many other commentators, believes that Jung abandoned the libido theory and sacrificed the truth of the sexual model in favor of a mystical/occult model. This shift away from the sexual model, Loewald believes, was the cause of the split between Freud and Jung. While this is certainly an aspect of the conflict that developed, it does not appear to be the complete story. Nor does it explain why these two very different men came together in the first place.

The theoretical dimensions that separated Freud and Jung might be organized into the following categories: the conflict over the universality of Oedipal dynamics, the inability of Jung to accept the theory of sexual etiology in neurosis, and divergence on the idea of libido.

Libido

Marilyn Nagy (1991) a Jungian Analyst and scholar from San Francisco traces the differences between the Jungian and Freudian conceptions of libido to the question of intentionality in her book Philosophical Issues in the Psychology of C. G. Jung. For Freud, libido was sexual in nature and as such reflected the central organizing factor in normal and neurotic functioning. Nagy asserts that Freud's conception of sexuality as central to normal functioning had at its core a view that the sexual libido was anchored in biological processes.

Nagy outlines the divergence of Jung from Freud's theory as occurring in the 1912 work by Jung, The Psychology of the Unconscious, later named, Symbols of Transformation. In this work, Nagy suggests, as mentioned in Chapter Three, that Jung conceived of libido as more than just sexual in order to account for the meaningful fantasies of schizophrenic patients. In this view, fantasy occurs with the regression of libido to the archaic strata of the mind which in turn produces symbols aiming at a healing function. At this time, Nagy (1991) states, "Jung began to speak of the progression of libido as purposive (p. 137). Jung, Nagy states, goes on to say

> I think that we should view with philosophic admiration the strange paths of the libido and should investigate its circuitous ways. It is not too much to say that we have herewith dug up the erotic root, and yet the problem remains unsolved. Were there not bound up with that *a mysterious purpose*, probably of the greatest biological meaning, then certainly twenty centuries would not have yearned for it with such intense longing. (p. 138)

Sexuality

Freud believed sexuality to be at the heart of neurosis. In his study of Dora he states (1901)

> I was anxious to show that sexuality does not simply intervene like a deus ex machina, on one single occasion...but that it provides the motive power for every single symptom, and for every single manifestation of a symptom...I can only repeat over and over—for I never find it otherwise—that sexuality is the key to the problem of psychoneuroses and of the neuroses in general. (p. 114)

In contrast to this was Jung's (1948) formulation that the "sexual dynamic is only one particular instance in the total field of the psyche. This is not to deny its existence, but merely to put it into its proper place" (p. 30). Even as early as 1906 and 1907 Jung held views that were supportive of Freud but with reservations. For instance, in his foreword to Psychology of Dementia Praecox in 1907 Jung states

> Even a superficial glance at my work will show how much I am indebted to the brilliant discoveries of Freud. As Freud has not yet received the recognition and appreciation he deserves, but is still opposed even in the most authoritative circles, I hope I may be allowed to define my position toward him...I can assure you that in the beginning I naturally entertained all the objections that are customarily made against Freud in the literature. But, I told myself, Freud could be refuted only by one who has made repeated use of the psychoanalytic method and who really investigates as Freud does; that is, by one who has made a long and patient study of everyday life, hysteria, and dreams from Freud's point of view. He who does not or cannot do this should not pronounce judgment on Freud, else he acts like those notorious men of science who disdained to look through Galileo's telescope. (para. 238)

In this statement we can see a scientific open-mindedness and a call for fairness. But in the following sentence, Jung reinforced his scientific stance tempered with an acknowledgement of his clinical experience and subjectivity. He states

> Fairness to Freud, however, does not imply, as many fear, unqualified submission to a dogma; one can very well maintain an independent judgment. If I, for instance, acknowledge the complex mechanisms of dreams and hysteria, this does not mean that I attribute to the infantile sexual trauma the exclusive importance that Freud apparently does. Still less does it mean that I place sexuality so predominantly in the foreground or that I grant it the psychological universality.
> (para 238)

Jung expresses this difference in perspective in his 1954 work on the etiology of neurosis in The Development of Personality.

Neurosis is a defense against the objective inner activity of the psyche...
to escape from the inner voice and hence from the vocation. Behind
the neurotic perversion is concealed [our] vocation, [our] destiny: the
growth of the personality, the full realization of the life-will that is
born with the individual. (para. 313)

That these differences are related to the underlying distinction between
Jung's emphasis on the purposive and Freud's stress on the reductive is supported by Charet (1993) who states "Jung's own feeling was that he could not
tolerate reducing all psychological disorders to repressed sexuality and not
consider their purposiveness which could render them therapeutic and not
merely pathological" (p. 179).

Oedipal or Heroic

Following from the ideas on sexuality emerge the two central myths
that mark the difference between Freud and Jung. Occurring during the
years between 1911 and 1913 both Freud and Jung sought to understand the
central myth of the human condition. Freud found this in the myth of Oedipus and Jung in the numerous myths of the hero struggling for deliverance.
In the Jungian formulation, the hero seeks to deliver the maiden from the
grips of the beast and in this way delivers himself from an internal unconsciousness.

It is here postulated that the difference in these two mythological formulations, like the difference in understanding the nature of libido and sexuality hinges upon the same basic distinction between Freud and Jung: the
question of intentionality and purpose in the psyche. Oedipus as written by
Sophocles begins with a glance to the past. Something has happened, and a
cause must be found.

Jung's mythological formula, however, is built differently. The hero
seeks deliverance and salvation by slaying the dragon and gaining freedom;
this was an expression of the struggle of an individual seeking deliverance
from the mother/unconscious. Jung states that he first encountered this phenomenon through observing the symbolic productions of the schizophrenic.
In Jung's model, the regressive tendency of the libido in schizophrenia has a
purpose, to aid in deliverance, to produce a symbol of potentiality, to work
for the future development of the individual. This model came to be known

as individuation. Jung (1916) used this term to refer to the process of coming to "selfhood" (p. 173).

Nagy refers to this process as a confrontation with the unconscious whereby the individual becomes him- or herself through differentiation revealed in the symbolic productions arising from the unconscious. In Jung's view, the implications of psychological incest, as in the Oedipal drama, were not necessarily sexual, but represented the vicissitudes of symbolic merger and separation. In this symbolic process, libido is freed from the symbolic merger to create the future life of the individual in the form of newly generated and understood meanings.

Further Reflection on the Relationship of Freud and Jung

Freud and Jung emerged out of opposing philosophical traditions, seeking different ends, and developing theories that reinforced the polarity between the rational and the irrational, the scientific and the spiritual, the archeological and the teleological. These differences were in existence prior to their meeting and yet they still sought each other out and spent seven years in one of the most powerful collaborations in psychoanalytic history.

One possible meaning of this phenomenon is that Freud and Jung were part of a larger movement bringing together these two men as manifestations of a tension that has existed throughout the course of psychodynamic psychotherapy.

Cultural Influence: The Origins of Dynamic Psychotherapy

Ellenberger (1970) expresses the tension emerging at the turn of the century as a struggle of modern dynamic psychotherapy to differentiate itself from religious, "irrational" ideas of healing. Ellenberger (1970) states, "Claude Levi-Strauss vigorously emphasized the basic identity of certain age-old concepts of primitive medicine to certain new concepts of modern dynamic psychiatry" (p. 6). This view contradicts the theory that our modern methods of therapeutic healing begin with Freud and are purely scientific as opposed to the occult or religious healing practices of the pre-Freudian era. Ellenberger notes the parallels that exist between primitive and modern methods of psychotherapeutic healing by stating

Among all primitive disease theories none is stranger to us than the idea of soul loss. And yet if we ignore the cultural element and seek the roots of facts, we may find a common ground between those primitive concepts and ours. Do we not say that our mental patients are 'alienated,' estranged from themselves, that their ego is impoverished or destroyed? Could not the therapist who gives psychotherapy to a severely deteriorated schizophrenic patient by trying to establish a contact with the remaining parts of the personality and to reconstruct the ego be considered a modern successor to the shamans who set out to follow the tracks of a lost soul, trace it into the world of spirits, and fight against the malignant demons detaining it, and bring it back to the world of the living. (p. 9)

These parallels reveal that the distinctions between the rational scientific method and the irrational primitive method is not as clear as many in psychoanalysis would like to believe. As Gallant (1996) states, "At the heart of the dismissals of Jung is the satisfied feeling that the exclusion is justified because his method was not based on 'science' as Freud's was" (p. 25). Following this idea, Homans, (1989) tells us that the need to identify with a scientific rather than a religious profession directly influences the psychoanalyst's willingness to entertain theoretical ideas that border on religion.

When the history of dynamic psychotherapy is examined with an eye to this question of science versus religion, it becomes clear that the tension between these opposites has always been at play (Charet, 1993). Out of this varied past we find a history of psychotherapeutic healing that contains elements of both these cultural forces. Freud was not the first to bring science to bear on psychodynamic healing and psychoanalysis is not exclusively scientific. This is important to our study in establishing that long before Freud and Jung began to develop their individual theories these two very different forces, the rational and irrational, the scientific and the religious, both existed in some varying configuration of tension and balance.

Homans (1989) states that "these two spaces, science and religion, provide the key to the social and cognitive location of psychoanalysis" (p. 342). From the basic notion that the development of psychoanalysis was part of a larger cultural movement in which science and religion have been variously related (Ellenberger, 1970; Charet, 1993) we can establish that this movement intensified in the 18th and 19th centuries in a force that was driving society away from religion toward science. This cultural movement has been referred to as secularization and elaborately detailed by the German philosopher Hans Blumenberg in The Legitimacy of the Modern Age (1983). This view has been applied to psychoanalysis by Homans (1989) where he states "a theory of secularization is essential for a more complete understanding of the origins of psychoanalysis, because only it fully recognizes and then explains the riddle or mystery of how a scientific view of the world, upon which psychoanalysis is predicated, could and did emerge from a religious one" (p. 314). In the simplest terms, secularization in this context can be defined as a shift from an understanding of the world through religious ideas to an understanding of the world through the human capacity for reason. Blumenberg (1983) traces a large arc in this process beginning with early Gnostic ideas and moving to medieval Catholic theology, the struggles of the seventeenth century, into the Enlightenment, Romanticism, and culminating in the person of Freud. This, Homans (1989) believes, shifted us from a religious view of the world as already finished to a scientific view of the world as unknown but capable of being known through human effort.

Understanding the Difference
Analysis and Synthesis

Homans (1978) refers to the difference in approach between Freud and Jung as applied to style and theory as culture-making for Jung versus culture-analyzing for Freud. For Homans, Freud was not concerned with how we create something new, but with understanding how we have been created from something old. This difference is expanded by Mark Kuras, a Jungian analyst, who formulates the difference as archeological for Freud and teleological for Jung. In relation to symbols and symptoms, he states (2000)

> There is the reductive approach, which is Freud's way, taking the symptom from the present back into the past, back to a repression, where "reality" was obscured. There is the synthetic way, Jung's, where the presence of the symptom is not a relic of the past, but the inscription of the faint struggle of a desire seeking, out ahead, its most deep articulation. (p. 32)

Both Homans and Kuras are approaching an aspect of our work that forms into the opposites of analysis and synthesis. Guntrip (1994) discusses this difference when he stresses that psychoanalysis is a tool for uncovering, but not for healing. He states

> It is now apparent that in practice psycho-analysis only has value as an instrument of scientific research into the painful areas of unconscious feeling and impulse...[but] the therapeutic factor is to be found in the object relationship of the patient and therapist. (p. 64)

Jung (1916a) in his initial work on dreams <u>General Aspects of Dream Psychology</u> refers to this by saying "All psychological phenomena have some such sense of purpose in them even merely reactive phenomena like emotional reactions" (p. 241). In this same paper Jung states, "Everywhere the question of the 'why' and 'wherefore' must be raised, because every organic structure consists of a complicated network of purposive functions" (p. 243).

As early as 1911 Jung was aware of this dimension in clinical material obtained in his work with schizophrenics. Jung (1912) states

> Thus, in so far as tomorrow is already contained in today, and all the threads of the future are already laid down, a deeper knowledge of the present might render possible a possibly far-sighted prognosis of the future...it seems as if from time to time, under certain conditions, important fragments of this work come to light, at least in dreams, thus accounting for the prophetic significance of dreams long claimed by superstition. (pp. 50-51)

One of the most cogent statements on the relevance of the purposive as a factor in the Freud/Jung split is found in one of Jung's letters to Freud from 1909. In commenting on an unusual spiritualistic occurrence with a patient Jung states

> I had the feeling that under it all there must be some quite special complex, a universal one having to do with the prospective tendencies in man. If there is a 'psychoanalysis' then there must also be a 'psychosynthesis' which creates future events according to the same laws... (McGuire, 1974, p. 215)

Frank Faranda

Mastery and Surrender

The idea of surrender, a relinquishing of ego authority, is a troublesome concept within the Western context of autonomy and self-reliance (Kuras, 2000). Unlike Eastern cultures where conceptions of the self are not based on individuality but rather on collectivity, surrender is more easily acceptable. So too in religious traditions, the notion of surrender finds an easier complementarity.

Any approach to a psychological understanding of surrender requires a look at both the subject and object of surrender. It also, by necessity, leads us to explore the implicit values on both the ego and the unconscious.

In coming to understand the subject and object of surrender, Kuras (2000) describes the difference in approach as a shift in perspective from viewing the ego as the center of the personality to viewing the Self as the center of the personality. He states that this difference can be understood as "seeing the unconscious as a teleological escort toward selfhood" (p. 31) and he goes on to discuss why this process is so threatening to classical psychoanalysis. He states (2000)

> Psychologically understood, it seems that to really move close to "Jung" is threatening because the point of view he offers really involves a letting go: shifting "I live" to "It lives me." (p. 31)

Fromm (1950) discusses the relationship of surrender to religion and to Jung's view of the unconscious. He states

> ...the essence of religious experience is the submission to powers higher than ourselves. But we had better quote Jung directly. He states that religion 'is a careful and scrupulous observation of what Rudolph Otto aptly termed the numinosum, that is a dynamic existence or effect, not caused by an arbitrary act of will. On the contrary, *it seizes and controls the human subject which is always rather its victim than its creator'* Having defined religious experience as being seized by a power outside ourselves, Jung proceeds to interpret the concept of the unconscious as being a religious one. (p. 17)

From this follows the implicit conceptions of valuation placed upon the unconscious. Phillip Rieff, Benjamin Franklin Professor of Sociology at the Uni-

82

versity of Pennsylvania, has written extensively on psychoanalysis and culture. In his 1987 book, <u>The Triumph of the Therapeutic</u> he states, "In the Jungian dialectic that ignored savior is the Unconscious itself, in one personification or another, come to correct the intellectual arrogance of consciousness" (p. 116). Jung (1934) speaks to this issue in the following

> The charge has recently been laid at my door that my teaching about the assimilation of the unconscious would undermine civilization and deliver up our highest values to sheer primitivity. Such an opinion can only be based on the erroneous supposition that the unconscious is a monster. It is a view that springs from fear of nature and the realities of life. Freud invented the idea of sublimation to save us from the imaginary claws of the unconscious. (para. 328)

In these words we find some useful clarification. Jung clearly states that psychoanalysis, beginning with Freud, ascribes a demonic character to the unconscious. He also acknowledges the fear that if we turn a face toward this "demon", surrender if you will, then our highest values will be lost. This combination makes understandable the fear of psychological surrender. But it is important to remember that Jung believed that the unconscious looks on us with the same face we turn to it.

Suspicion and Faith

Joseph Newirth (2001) has outlined three epistemological structures at work in our psychoanalytic culture. He states

> From a historical and philosophical perspective there seem to be three independent epistemological structures, three alternative and equally valid sets of assumptions about how we generate knowledge, about the nature of the world, what constitutes knowing and our understanding of what it means to be a person. (p. 11)

The simplicity of this formulation brings into clear relief the differences that this essay is highlighting. In Newirth's view, each of these models is equal in value but different in meaning. The three structures he proposes are the Discourse of Faith, Love, and Religion; the Discourse of Science, Positivism, and Modernism; and the Discourse of Literature, Art, and Postmodernism.

Phillip Rieff (1987) speaks about Jung's psychology as a language of faith. Initially he states that "as Jung well knew, all modes of faith appear slightly fraudulent in an age of science" (p. 109).

Eigen (1981) links faith to a non-defensive stance. He states, "Faith as a fundamental dimension is in tension with the defensive use of mastery..." (p. 432). He goes on to say, "By area of faith I mean to point to a way of experiencing which is undertaken with one's whole being, all out, with all one's heart, with all one's soul, and with all one's might" (p. 413). In these statements we can note the tension with science. Bion (1977) speaks of this area of experience when he states

> It may be wondered what state of mind is welcomed if desires and memories are not. A term that would express approximately what I need to express is 'faith'—faith that there is an ultimate reality and truth. (p. 31)

Mark Wallace (1995) in his introduction to Paul Ricoeur's book Figuring the Sacred discusses the links of faith to teleology. He states

> In a dialectical spirit of his aborted poetics of the will, Ricoeur contends that an archeology of the decentered subject should stand in tension with a teleology of the fulfilled subject that takes seriously, though not literally, childhood dreams, works of art, and religious symbols as lived possibilities for a transformative future. (p. 7)

An Essential Difference

Marilyn Nagy (1991) formulates her understanding of the difference in what is Jungian in relation to the question of positivism. For Freud, positivism was at the center of his worldview. In such a positivist system of philosophy, theology and metaphysics belong to an earlier more imperfect mode of knowledge. Nagy states that in contrast to this, for Jung, the tradition of vitalism governed his outlook, his theory, and ultimately his clinical practice. Vitalism holds that there is a tendency in an organism moving it toward an achievement of maturity. Tracing this Jungian orientation back to the teleological perspectives of Plato and Aristotle, Nagy states

> The teleological edifice erected by Plato and Aristotle—a world view which regarded all of nature as a developmental process headed toward the final goals of a transcendent being—remained in its main structure unchallenged until the end of the nineteenth century. (p. 113)

Jung valued the idea of vitalism as far back as his university days. In the Zofingia Lectures, the series of lectures mentioned earlier, he states (1896)

> The vital principle extends far beyond our consciousness in that it also maintains the vegetative functions of the body which, as we know, are not under our conscious control. Our consciousness is dependent on the functions of the brain, but these are in turn dependent on the vital principle, and accordingly the vital principle represents a substance, whereas consciousness represents a contingent phenomenon. (para 96)

By stating that the vital principal is a substance, Jung was metaphorically giving objective existence to this governing pattern of development. In contrast to this, consciousness, Jung argues, represents a subjective phenomenon rather than a structural entity. Jung, according to Nagy, developed a neo-vitalist perspective that underlies his entire model of the mind.

Conclusion

In this chapter, the Freud/Jung relationship has been explored from a variety of vantage points to reveal similarities, differences, and contextual dimensions. And although psychoanalysis is no longer even remotely synonymous with what is Freudian, it is postulated that there are perhaps unconscious remnants of this relationship along with unresolved difficulties with religious and spiritual ideas that makes it hard to formulate theory on the psyche as purposive. This supports the previously illuminated patterns that emerged in the theory of the self and the theory of dreams. Together, these data illuminate a correlation between the undeveloped theory of the Purposive Self and the absence of Jung from the psychoanalytic dialogue.

Chapter Five: The Purposive in the Jungian Model and Applied Clinical Concepts

In this chapter we will explore more deeply the elements of the Jungian model of the mind that support the theoretical construct of a Purposive Self. As already noted, these elements form the essential difference between Freudian Psychoanalysis and Jungian Analysis. That this distinction is not absolute was seen in Chapter Two where psychological conceptualizations of the self emerging out of psychoanalytic theory were seen to approach, approximate, and struggle with elements supporting a model for a Purposive Self. These areas of overlap were specifically in the domains of the *Self as Core* and the *Self as Process*. Chapter Three on dream theory and use revealed that subsequent to Freud's original paradigm, a shift in the interpretive use of dreams took place that focused on the manifest dream, in varying ways, as a meaningful representation and not a disguise. It was also seen that the developments toward this clinical usage were not accompanied by the development of an adequate model of dream theory. What was lost was the power of Freud's metapsychology in explaining why the dream exists and what forces were responsible for its production. In this way, the elements of the Jungian model of the mind being explored in this chapter might be considered a revision of Freud's metapsychology.

The presentation of Jungian ideas in this chapter is not intended to be a complete picture of Jungian theory; rather it is a selective offering of ideas on the Purposive Self that can complement a psychodynamic view of human experience by expanding and clarifying already existent theoretical frames of reference (Beebe et al., 2001).

Elements of the Jungian Model of the Mind that Support the Purposive Self
    The Self
As with psychoanalytic theories of the self, it is often difficult to separate the Jungian formulations referring to the core of the self from the formu-

lations referring to the processes of the self. The *Self as Core* is often viewed as the blueprint or potential for the self as distinct from the *Self as Process* that acts to unfold this developmental design. In the Jungian model, the Self is both a center within the unconscious paralleling the ego and the manifestation of that center through the processes of individuation that bring about the balance of opposites, the work toward wholeness, and the functioning of the dream and symbolic experience.

The overlap of *Core* and *Process* within the Jungian model is found in the conceptualization of Andrew Samuels (2000) where he refers to the Self as the "intelligence in the unconscious" (p. 408). Neumann (1996) refers to this as the ego-self axis where psychic functioning is represented by the interplay of the conscious and the unconscious within the personality. In each of these ideas is the overlap of *Core* and *Process*. This is evidenced in the evocation of the somewhat archaic concept of entelechy. This concept moves beyond the notion of mere seed to the unfolding of the seed. From Aristotle it is implied that the cause of the form is already fully realized. This is a step beyond mere potential in that it implies completion and a function to bring about this development. To the Vitalists, of whom Jung numbered, entelechy was something that contained both an end and an agency to directs the progress toward that end.

The Archetype

A link in understanding the Jungian differentiation of *Core* and *Process* resides in what Jung called the archetype. Jung (1949) states that the archetype is "an inherited mode of psychic functioning, corresponding to the inborn way in which the chick emerges from the egg, the bird builds its nest" (para. 1229). In this statement Jung envisions the archetype as the pattern into which life unfolds. This might be similar to Chomsky's (1968) "deep structures" or Klein's (1932) concept of the "inherited breast." Jung (1942) expresses a further metaphor when he states, "They [archetypes] may be compared to the invisible presence of the crystal lattice in a saturated solution... the biological pattern of behavior which gives all living organisms their specific qualities" (p. 222n). And in Aion (1951) Jung continues the allusions to physics in stating

Sooner or later nuclear physics and the psychology of the unconscious will draw closer together as both of them, independently of one another and from opposite directions, push forward into transcendental territory, the one with the concept of the atom, the other with that of the archetype. (p. 412)

It is clear that Jung believes that the archetype is the base material, "prima material" in his alchemical world, and that it has an actual basis in reality even though at present it is not possible to perceive it. This parallels the early scientific certainty about the atom or DNA regardless of the ability to directly perceive them.

The archetypal background of a person is a difficult concept to conceive of for a number of reasons. The relationship of this concept to questions of innate endowment, infancy, instincts, development, and the impact of the environment is quite complex. This complexity notwithstanding, Jung (1940) argues that "archetypes were, and still are, living psychic forces that demand to be taken seriously, and they have a strange way of making sure of their effect" (p. 266).

Although largely neglecting issues of infancy and childhood, Jung believes that the psyche of the newborn child is hardly a tabula rasa (Jung 1936). There is something quite modern, similar to Stern (1985), in Jung's conceptualization of the infant. Jung states (1936)

In so far as the infant is born with a differentiated brain that is predetermined by heredity and therefore individualized, it meets sensory stimuli coming from outside not with *any* aptitudes, but with *specific* ones and this necessarily results in a particular, individual choice and pattern of apperception...their presence gives the world of the child and the dreamer its anthropormorphic stamp. *They are the archetypes, which direct all fantasy activity into its appointed paths*...(ibid, p. 136, italics mine)

It is clear that Jung believes that the archetypes are patterns and templates that help the infant and child to understand and organize what is perceived. The connection to Stern's research lies in the competency that Jung ascribes to the mind of the infant. There is also contained in these words the understanding that the archetypes, through their template-like ability to aid in the apperception of the environment, are like physiological "organs of the pre-rational psyche" (Jung, 1935, p.845). A further link to development can be seen when Jung (1935) states

> They [the archetypes] are eternally inherited forms and ideas which at first have no specific content. Their specific content only appears in the course of the individual's life, when personal experience is taken up in precisely these forms. (p. 845)

Individuation—the Self as Process

Extending beyond the already explored and somewhat hesitant theoretical formations from the psychoanalytic community on the *Self as Process* are the explicit Jungian conceptualizations of individuation. These appear specifically in Jungian literature dealing with the function of dreams, the formation of dreams, the innate healing potential of the psyche, the regulatory process for affective experience, the balancing of one-sidedness, the processes of development over the lifespan, and the search for authenticity.

In approaching the Jungian idea of the *Self as Process* manifesting as individuation, the central idea to come away with is that the process of individuation is a process whereby the person becomes an individual. This is a process that takes place in a delicate balance with nature. On the one hand, Jung proposes that something within the *Core* of a person propels that person toward uniqueness, and on the other hand, Jung envisions a tendency in nature to remain uniform and collective. For Jungians, analysis strives to enable the conscious participation in the process of individuation: becoming a unique person, separate, yet related to the underlying collective community.

Individuation as a concept surfaced for the first time in Jung's 1913 paper "A Contribution to the Study of Psychological Types" delivered while Jung was still president of the International Psychoanalytic Association and still associated with Freud. This conference marked the last time the two men met in person. That the emergence of this concept, one so central to Jungian Analytical thought and one that also marks a primary point of divergence of Jung from Freudian psychoanalysis, occurred at the point when the split between these two men became manifest, is not without significance. As explored in Chapter Four, the purposive constitutes an essential difference that becomes manifest theoretically, clinically, politically and philosophically. Individuation is the expression of this difference as a function of the psyche.

For Jung, the reference to individuation occurs as Jung (1913) attempts to contrast the extraverted character type from the introverted character type. In his illucidation, Jung gives reference to Nietzsche's (1909) use the terms Apollonian and Dionysian. Jung states that Nietzsche expressed the contrast between these two qualities of being as similar to the contrast of a dream and an intoxication. Jung (1913) states, "In the dream an individual is shut up in himself, it is the most intimate of all psychic experiences; in intoxication he is liberated from himself, and utterly self-forgotten" (p. 506). Jung then traces Nietzsche's usage of the term Apollonian to Schopenhauer (1883)

> As upon a tumultuous sea, unbounded in every direction, the mariner sits full of confidence in his frail barque, rising and falling amid the raging mountains of waves, so the individual man, in a world of troubles, sits passive and serene, trusting to the *principium individuationis.* (p. 455)

Nietzsche (1909) goes on to say, "Yes, one might say that the unshakable confidence in this principle [principium individuationis] and the calm security of those whom it has inspired, have found in Apollo their most sublime expression, and one might describe Apollo himself as the glorious divine image of the principle of individuation" (p. 125). Jung (1913) extends this to the idea of character type by stating, "The Apllonian state, therefore, as Nietzsche conceives it, is a withdrawal into oneself, or introversion" (p. 507).

From these initial ideas present at the origin of the concept, one can detect many of the seeds for all future elaborations. Important elements that will surface in the course of this enquiry are: 1.) this is a principle found in nature; 2.) there is a movement toward the inner regions of the unconscious; 3.) that one must trust the principle and sit serene "amid a torrent;" 4.) that this process is similar to a voyage.

Jung (1921) describes individuation as "the process by which individual beings are formed and differentiated" (p. 448). He goes on to say, "Individuation, therefore, is a process of differentiation having for its goal the development of the individual personality" and "Individuation is always to some extent opposed to collective norms" (p. 448). Relating the idea to development he states, "Individuation is practically the same as the development of consciousness out of the original state of identity" (p. 449). Edinger (1984), one of Jung's classical followers, expresses quite clearly the urge and aim of individuation when he states, "Motivated by the autonomous urge to individuation...the ego must strive to know the Self and to realize it consciously" (p. 109). That the Self is a goal and not a concrete reality is elaborated by Whitmont (1969)

> Individuation is always a road, a way, a process, travel or travail, a dynamism; it is never, at least not while one life's in time and space, a static of accomplished state. It is 'becoming,' not 'being.' The Self as the 'goal' of the individuation process may be likened to the pole star: one may plot one's course by it, but one does not expect to reach it. (pp. 221-222)

And in quite simple language Jung (1939) states, "I use the term "individuation" to denote a process by which a person becomes a psychological "individual," that is, a separate indivisible unity or "whole" (p. 275).

One of the ideas that emerges in this discussion of Jung's concept of individuation is the relation of this process to the notion of fate. In discussing the impact of the moments of fate in a person's life, Jung (1945) states

> All these moments in the individual's life, when the universal laws of human fate break in upon the purposes, expectations, and opinions of the personal consciousness, are stations along the road of the individuation process. This process is, in effect, the spontaneous realization of the whole man...since everything living strives for wholeness, the inevitable one-sidedness of our conscious life is continually being corrected and compensated by the universal human being in us, whose goal is the ultimate integration of conscious and unconscious, or better, the assimilation of the ego to a wider personality. (p. 292)

In this statement is the notion that everything in nature strives for wholeness. This is akin to an instinctual drive that has a single purpose and aim. As already noted, this idea emerges in part from Jung's Vitalist philosophical foundations. Jung also states that the process of individuation is spontaneous. A further idea is that this process is directed by the "universal human being" whose goal is integration and "assimilation of the ego to a wider personality." In this there is the implication that some personified inner intelligence is directing the process of growth. But what is most salient in this statement, is the idea that the process of individuation happens naturally and without conscious participation.

In Jung's formulation, fate is something that the conscious individual can participate in as an aspect of an inner process, and not simply experience as something happening from outside. Whitmont (1969) conveys this paradoxical position through quoting an old Roman proverb: "Whoever is willing, the Fates will lead, the unwilling they will drag along" (p. 48).

The obvious implication of this complex idea of fate is that the process of individuation can take place in one of two ways: by mandate or by consent, but that, either way, it will take place. From this emerges the notion of similarity of both process and goal. In other words, both the natural fateful process and the consciously participated process would be striving in the same direction toward the same goal. That this is not altogether certain is revealed in Jung's oft quoted dictum that "individuation is an opus contra naturam" (Jung, 1939, p. 146). What requires clarification is the idea that consciousness, the product of individuation, is set against a natural unconsciousness. In individuation, nature becomes aware of itself. It is important, however, to make note that simply because individuation is an innate process of nature, does not guarantee its fulfillment. Developmental experience, trauma, illness, and even certain levels of choice, can interfere with, and disrupt the individuation process.

Adding to the confusion surrounding individuation, is the often stated assignation of higher value for the consciously participated in path as opposed to the state of natural being. This is evidenced in Whitmont (1969) when he states that Jung believed that human freedom was only grounded in the choice made to walk "on our appointed path" (Jung, 1948, para 746). Jung (1948) states

> Natural man is not a 'self'—he is the mass and the particle in the mass, collective to such a degree that he is not even sure of his own ego...and that amounts to spiritual death. Life that just happens in and for itself is not real life, it is only real when it is known. Only a unified person can experience life, not that personality that is split up into partial aspects, that bundle of odds and ends which also calls itself "man." (para 104-105)

Frank Faranda

Adding to this understanding is Whitmont's (1969) statement that individuation is a "conscious striving for becoming what one 'is' or rather, what one 'is meant to be.'" (p. 221). It is the "conscious striving" that is being isolated as a particular way in which individuation is conceptualized and, thus, in turn, as a particular way in which the psyche organizes and manifests as a human life.

Edinger (1984) adds an important element in his understanding of conscious participation by stating

> The hallmark of individuation is the *differentiation* of the individual psyche from its containment in the collective psyche. (p. 85)

Jung's ideas in this area related to individuation as a separation from the collective psyche touch upon an important element in the Jungian model of the mind. Jung (1935) speaks to the relationship of the collective to the personal

> In addition to our immediate consciousness which is of a thoroughly personal nature and which we believe to be the only empirical psyche...there exists a second psychic system of a collective, universal, and impersonal nature which is identical in all individuals. This collective unconscious does not develop individually but is inherited. It consists of pre-existent forms, the archetypes, which can only become conscious secondarily and which give definite form to certain psychic contents. (pp. 43-44)

In speaking of the process of differentiation of the individual from the collective, Jung (1921) notes, "the antithesis of the collective is the individual" (p. 418), and

> Although biological instinctive processes contribute to the formation of personality, individuality is nevertheless essentially different from collective instincts; indeed, it stands in the most direct opposition to them, just as the individual as a personality is always distinct from the collective. His essence consists precisely in this distinction. (ibid, p. 88)

In these statements we see that the individual is recognized as an achievement over the collective and that the individual is essentially at odds with the collective values. The antagonistic nature of the relationship of the collective and the individual is noted in the following from Jung (1928)

> The element of differentiation is the individual. All the highest achievements of virtue, as well as the blackest villainies, are individual. The larger the community is, and the more the sum total of collective factors peculiar to every large community rests on conservative prejudices detrimental to individuality, the more the individual will be morally and spiritually crushed, and as a result, the one source of moral and spiritual progress for society is choked up. Naturally, the only thing that can thrive in such an atmosphere is sociality and whatever is collective in the individual. Everything individual in him goes under, i.e. is doomed to repression. (p. 240)

Again it is important to remember that Jung postulates the parallel between the collective within the psyche and the collective values within society. He comments on this relationship (1928)

> Human beings have one faculty which though it is of the greatest utility for collective purposes, is the most pernicious for individuation, and that is the faculty of imitation. Collective psychology cannot dispense with imitation, for without it all mass organizations, the State and the social order, are impossible. Society is organized, indeed, less by law than by the propensity to imitation, implying equally suggestibility, suggestion, and mental contagion. But we see everyday how people use, or rather abuse, the mechanism of imitation for the purpose of personal differentiation: they are content to ape some eminent personality, some striking characteristic or mode of behavior, thereby achieving an outward distinction from the circle in which they move. We could almost say that as a punishment for this the uniformity of their minds with those of their neighbors already real enough, is intensified into an unconscious, compulsive bondage to the environment. As a rule these specious attempts at individual differentiation stiffen into a pose, and the imitator remains at the same level as he always was, only several degrees more sterile than he was before. (p. 242)

The final offering from Jung (1928) on the collective and its apparent negative effect on the individual expresses the precariousness of the individuation process

Frank Faranda

> On closer examination one is always astonished to see how much our
> so-called individual psychology is really collective. So much, indeed,
> that the individual traits are completely overshadowed by it. Since,
> however, individuation is an ineluctable psychological necessity, we
> can see from the ascendancy of the collective what very special atten-
> tion must be paid to this very delicate plant 'individuality' if it is not
> to be completely smothered. (p. 241)

The Nature of Psychic Energy and its Relationship to Symbolic Activity

In order to full apprehend the Purposive Self within a psychodynamic
model of the mind and the dream as manifestation of this self it is necessary
to make explicit an understanding of the nature of psychic energy. For Jung,
psychic energy is not specifically tied to the drives of sex and aggression.
Rather, he views libido as a general source of energy for the functioning of the
psyche. A second element in the Jungian model of libido is the understanding
of psychic energy as directly linked to the expression of symbolic material
(Whitmont, 1969). For Jung, the psyche is inherently imagistic and it is for
this reason that the dream is essentially a communication through images.

Jung, in his later work, adopts the term, *objective psyche,* to specify the
level of the unconscious psyche from which these images emerge. As Whitmont (1969) states

> What Jung calls the objective psyche may be likened to an encom-
> passing energy stratum from which arise…the patternings of image,
> emotion, and drive configurations. (p. 42)

Out of these patternings come the various forms present in the symbolic fantasies and dreams observable in clinical material. As Jung states (1928)

> Libido can never be apprehended except in a definite form; that is to
> say, it is identical with fantasy-images. (para. 345)

And applied to the general functioning of the *Self as Process* it is possible to
say that creativity, imagination, and play are all ways in which the mind can
function as distinct from conscious thinking. As Jung (1921) states, "fantasy as imaginative activity is identical with the flow of psychic energy" (pa-
ra.722).

96

The Dream

For most Jungians, the dream is of primary importance in a psychotherapeutic treatment. The reasons for this derive from the basic Jungian view that the dream is a clear representation of the unconscious "as it is," and that the dream offers a prospective view of what is required in terms of compensation and individuation (Samuels, 1985, 2000; Sedgewick, 2000). Jung has extensively outlined the nature, functioning, and interpretation of dreams. His understanding of the dream grows out of the clinical situation and is designed, not for theoretical certainty, but for therapeutic facility. Jung (1931) states

> I have no theory about dreams, I do not know how dreams arise. And I am not at all sure that my way of handling dreams even deserves the name of a 'method.' I share all your prejudices against dream interpretation as the quintessence of uncertainty and arbitrariness. On the other hand, I know that if we meditate on a dream sufficiently long and thoroughly, if we carry it around with us and turn it over and over, something almost always comes of it. This something is not of course a scientific result to be boasted about or rationalized; but it is an important practical hint which shows the patient what the unconscious is aiming at. Indeed it ought not to matter to me whether the result of my musings on the dream is scientifically verifiable or tenable, otherwise I am pursuing an ulterior—and therefore autoerotic—aim. I must content myself wholly with the fact that the result means something to the patient and sets his life in motion again. I may allow myself only one criterion for the result of my labours: does it work? As for my scientific hobby—my desire to know why it works—this I must reserve for my spare time. (p. 86)

From the above phenomenological perspective, the most salient aspect of the dream experience is its spontaneous production distinct from conscious control. As Jung (1920) expresses it

> We do not feel as if we are producing the dreams...they are not subject to our control but obey their own laws. They are obviously autonomous psychic complexes which form themselves out of their own material. We do not know the source of their motives, and we therefore say that dreams come from the unconscious. In saying this, we assume that

there are independent psychic complexes which elude our conscious control and come and go according to their own laws. (p. 580)

From observing the manifestations of this autonomous level of functioning, Jungians construct a psychological model containing a source within the unconscious that is capable of generating this spontaneous product: the Self.

The functioning of the dream, as understood by Jungians, manifests in two inter-related ways. It is both a natural corrective occurrence, a self-regulatory function of the *Self as Process,* and as a purposive occurrence, an individuation function of the *Self as Process.* As already noted, these two areas overlap in both form and function.

The primary functioning of the dream on the self-regulatory level is not directly tied to any kind of interpretation, understanding or even remembrance. The dream in this basic self-regulatory function is understood as a natural ongoing process whereby the psyche attempts to establish a balance between the conscious and the unconscious. Jung (1916a) states "dreams contribute to the self-regulation of the psyche by automatically bringing up everything that is repressed or neglected or unknown" (p. 483) and, "It is evident that this is a function of dreams that amounts to a psychological adjustment, a compensation absolutely necessary for properly balanced action" (ibid, p. 469). And finally, Jung (1963) expresses unequivocally his understanding of the self-regulatory function of the dream

> Lack of conscious understanding does not mean that the dream has no effect at all. Even civilized man can occasionally observe that a dream which he cannot remember can slightly alter his mood for better or worse. Dreams can be "understood" to a certain extent in a subliminal way, and that is mostly how they work. (p. 52)

The balance of opposites that Jungians speak of in this dialogue is expressed in a number of ways: attitudes, remembrances, attributions of meaning, values, and the splitting of internal objects. The self-regulation, then, takes the form of a dream that balances, perhaps, an overly manic conscious state by generating a dream image that would compensate by generating a depressive affect or reveal a memory in the unconscious that is being defended against and which when consciously acknowledged, effects a balancing of the conscious mood.

The second layer in a Jungian understanding of the dream moves beyond the natural self-regulatory, compensatory function, and speaks of the dream as a communication from the Self to the ego. This links to the earlier conceptualization of individuation as a process of conscious participation. To Jung, the dream is an utterance from the unconscious that attempts communication for a specific purpose. At each moment the Self is generating images in the dream that reach consciousness and alter personality through insight, assimilation, and integration. Jung (1933) states

> In each of us there is another whom we do not know. He speaks to us in dreams and tells us how differently he sees us from the way we see ourselves. When, therefore, we find ourselves in a difficult situation to which there is no solution, he can sometimes kindle a light that radically alters our attitude—the very attitude that led us into the difficult situation. (p. 325)

As in the above statement from Jung, and equally in other authors who approach this view of the dream, there is a tendency to personify the inner purposive functions of the Self. This is true in James Grotstein (2000) who conceives of the process as the inner "dreamer who dreams the dream," a subjective presence to whom one can assign responsibility for the formation of the dream.

The awareness that the dream is bringing together associations, memories, affects, ideas long forgotten, and weaving them together to form a symbolic meaning that will impact consciousness through the very fact of its production and experience is quite profound. Jung (1916a) expresses this complexity when he states

> If our dreams produce certain ideas these ideas are primarily our ideas, in the structure of which our whole being is interwoven. They are subjective factors, grouping as they do in the dream, and expressing this or that meaning, not for extraneous reasons but from the most intimate promptings of our psyche. The whole dreamwork is essentially subjective, and a dream is a theatre in which the dreamer is himself the scene, the player, the prompter, the producer, the author, the public, and the critic. (p. 509)

This same metaphor of the theater is used 84 years later by Grotstein (2000)

> Dreams are dramatic narratives written, directed, and produced by a composite dreamer who is unknown to us, who employs narrative as the instrument of phantasy and myth and uses Neurophysiological perception—namely visualization—to organize the chaotic fragmented accretions of mental pain left over as residues of yet one more day of existence. (p. 10)

In both these conceptualizations, there is the awareness that the dream is highly complex, requiring a multitude of functioning on a multitude of levels and that this process is beyond the conscious ability of the human being. In other words, understanding the dream as a function of an organized individuation process requires the acknowledgement that the creation and expression of the dream within that context are not reasonably understood as a product of the ego but as a more sophisticated functioning of the Purposive Self.

It is important to note that these conceptualizations are purely psychological and based on the dream as a clinical phenomenon. Jung never attempted to forge a neurobiological model to explain the formation of the dream.

Applications Within a Psychodynamic Treatment
  A Belief in Healing

The broadest description of the way in which the idea of a Purposive Self impacts treatment comes through the therapist's faith in the self-healing potential of the psyche. Whitmont (1969) states, "Jung credits the psyche with a potentiality toward self-healing. The idea that the unconscious contains also a healing potential and not only disturbing elements was one of Jung's unique and revolutionary discoveries" (p. 295). As already noted, many authors within psychoanalytic theory have approached this idea; Weiss (1986); Fosshage (1983, 2000); and Fromm (1951) are just a few. Jung elaborates this idea more fully and, from his perspective, the therapist more directly participates in this unique process. To Jung, the therapist is required to often defer to the Self in determining the course of healing. It was believed that through this deference an authentic path could be discovered. This acknowledgment and deference to the Self as authority in directing the innate healing process shifts the role of the therapist and imbues the analytic relationship with faith.

The Self of the Analyst

As noted by several authors, Jung was ahead of his time with regard to appreciating and valuing the mutuality of the analytic situation (Jacoby, 1990; Samuels, 2000). The basis for Jung's understanding of this importance stems from his view that the psyche is relationally influenced, not only consciously, but unconsciously as well. When Jung lectured in London in 1935 to a group of physicians and analysts (including Bion) he stated, "emotions of patients...are very contagious when the contents which the patient projects into the analyst are identical with the analyst's own unconscious contents" (Jung, 1935, p. 140). Jung believes that it is the duty of the analyst to "accept the emotions of the patient and to mirror them" (p. 139). Later Jung (1946) adds that analysts "could collect information of a psychological nature, not only from their patients but also from themselves, i.e., from the observation of their own unconscious contents which had been activated by induction," (p. 201) and Jung (1951) states "a good half of every treatment that probes at all deeply, consists in the doctor's examining himself, for only what he can put right in himself can he hope to put right in the patient" (p. 116).

These comments foreshadow Object Relations theory and the development of ideas on countertransference and projective identification (Ogden, 1986), relationally oriented psychoanalytic theory stressing mutuality (Greenberg & Mitchell, 1983), Kohut's model of empathy in treatment (Kohut, 1984), and the recent advances in infant developmental theory focusing on attunement and its application to adult treatment (Fosha, 2000).

Developmental Jungians who have integrated psychoanalytic theory into their practice offer a current understanding of these ideas as they apply to the role of the analyst. Sedgwick (2000) states, "the role of the analyst is central to treatment, in the form of the analyst's being an engaged participant, willing to be affected by the patient's problems, transference, or self" (p. 464). Zabriskie's (2000) conception of the analyst centers on the role of the mediator for the patient's inner world, "Attentive, reflective, and imaginal engagement aims toward therapeutic change through ongoing dialogue between ego and unconscious via the psychic conversation and the analytic dialogue" (p. 397). Kalsched (2000) states that these ideas on the role of the analyst were the reason Jung altered classical use of the couch in favor of a face-to-face model. This is done, according to Kalsched, to enhance the mutuality and empathic resonance and to orient the work to a third space between analyst and patient.

Samuels (1985, 2000) believes that the increased relational role of the analyst in the treatment process was the most important clinical contribution of Jung. Samuels extends this by exploring the unconscious-to-unconscious dimension of the analyst-patient dyad with the notion of the wounded healer. In this conception, the analyst remains aware of his or her own areas of illness so as to avoid attribution of these areas to the patient. Also important in this model is the acknowledgement that within the patient there is an internal healer which Jungians conceptualize as the Self.

Tending to the Self

As noted, Jung was not primarily concerned with infancy and early development, nor was he very practical in his outline of treatment and technique. Sedgwick (2000) states

> Jung, in my opinion, had brilliant things to say about psychotherapy, and some have suggested that his theory of complexes was the first object relations therapy. However, after he left the psychiatric clinic and the psychoanalytic movement, he did not go into much clinical detail. His descriptions of both therapy and transference concentrate on the symbolic, sometimes even alchemical imagery, which makes them intriguing but enigmatic. Therefore, the relative clinical concreteness of psychoanalytic thought is necessary to fill in the gaps. (p. 462)

Jacoby (2000) speaks to the same limitation in Jung's model when he states that the necessity of becoming more sophisticated about events in the analytic relationship "led me and several other Jungian colleagues over the past 20 or 30 years to familiarize ourselves with developments in psychoanalysis and to integrate them into Jung's embracing approach" (p. 495). In the 1970's Jacoby discovered a strong affinity for the ideas of Kohut and the use of an empathic stance in furthering psychological development.

From these ideas emerges the third important aspect that becomes explicit in integrating the purposive into a psychodynamic model of treatment: the parallel between the needs of the developing self in infancy and the needs of the Self in the ongoing process of individuation throughout adulthood. Infant developmental theory after Stern (1985) illuminated development as centered on the self and contingent upon attunement and empathy. This was an empirical validation of the ideas from Object Relations theorists such as Winnicott and Self Psychologists such as Kohut. Out of this model comes the basic view that empathy is ameliorative to early developmental difficulties. This way of working not only supports the repair of difficulties from infancy and childhood but also supports ongoing development of the Self.

In both the psychoanalytic and the Jungian ideas of the Self, the question of development, both restorative and ongoing, is a primary concern. The inclusion of psychoanalytic and infant developmental research on the Self and the needs of the Self have helped Jungians to better understand both the ways to heal developmental issues from childhood as well as further the ongoing development of the Self through the process of individuation.

As noted already, for Jungians, the Self's journey becomes manifest through the process of individuation and the maintenance of that journey arises through the function of dreaming.

The Use of the Dream

Jung's writings on the nature of the dream are often unequivocal and certain. His recommendations for the interpretation of dreams, however, are somewhat tempered and driven by clinical imperative and individual difference. Jung (1947) states

> So difficult is it to understand a dream that for a long time I have made it a rule, when someone tells me a dream and asks for my opinion, to say first of all to myself: "I have no idea what this dream means." After that I can begin to examine the dream. (p. 533)

Also unexpected, given the complexity and abstruse nature of Jung's understanding of the dream, is Jung's assertion that his work with dreams is not encumbered by theory

> I leave theory aside as much as possible when analyzing dreams—not entirely, of course, for we always need some theory to make things intelligible. It is on the basis of theory, for instance, that I expect dreams to have a meaning. I cannot prove in every case that this is so, for there are dreams which the doctor and the patient simply do not

103

understand. But I have to make such an hypothesis in order to find the courage to deal with dreams at all. (1934, p. 318)

Again in these words is the balance between clinical rigor and human limitation. For Jung, the essential relationship to the dream hinges upon this delicate balance and becomes manifest not through the brilliance of the intellect, but through the resonance of the whole person. Jung (1933) states

One would do well to treat every dream as though it were a totally unknown object. Look at it from all sides, take it in your hand, carry it about with you, let your imagination play round it ... (p. 320)

Jung's sense of play with the dream, however, has a framework and a set of clear assumptions. All the ideas on the nature and function of the dream that were explored up to this point in this chapter comprise the theoretical background of the analyst as he or she works with the dream. These are the basis for his or her hypotheses. What Jung is attempting to differentiate in these clinical remarks is that the use of the dream in treatment must be specific to the individual

The psychological context of dream-contents consists in the web of associations in which the dream is naturally embedded. Theoretically we can never know anything in advance about this web, but in practice it is sometimes possible, granted long enough experience. In the analysis of isolated dreams above all, this kind of knowing in advance and making assumptions on the grounds of practical expectation or general probability is positively wrong. It should therefore be an absolute rule to assume that every dream, and every part of a dream, is unknown at the outset, and to attempt an interpretation only after carefully taking up the context. (1944, p. 48)

Associations, and the associational web, as Jung refers to it, are essential in the Jungian model for dream interpretation; for each person the meaning of an image will have a slightly different variation. As Jung (1931) states

Seen purely theoretically, a dream image can mean anything or nothing. For that matter, does a thing or a fact ever mean anything in itself? The only certainty is that it is always man who interprets, who assigns meaning. And that is the gist of the matter of psychology. (p. 93)

Moving beyond isolated ideas on interpretation, Jung views the essential element in interpretation to be the patient's experience. He states (1934)

> It makes very little difference whether the doctor understands or not, but it makes all the difference whether the patient understands. Understanding should therefore be understanding in the sense of an agreement which is the fruit of a joint reflection. The danger of a one-sided understanding is that the doctor may judge the dream from the standpoint of a preconceived opinion. His judgment may be in line with orthodox theory, it may even be fundamentally correct, but it will not win the patient's assent, he will not come to an understanding with him, and that is in the practical sense incorrect—incorrect because it anticipates and thus cripples the patient's development. The patient, that is to say, does not need to have a truth inculcated into him—if we do that, we only reach his head; he needs far more to grow up to this truth, and in that way we reach his heart, and the appeal goes deeper and works more powerfully. (p. 314)

In the following chapter, the ideas presented here on the Jungian model will be used in conjunction with contemporary ideas of psychodynamic treatment to illustrate a potential area of integration.

Chapter Six: The Case of Nora

Nora called in late July to begin treatment at the university clinic. When I spoke to her initially she stated that she had some medical difficulties and her doctor suggested she try psychotherapy. We made an appointment for the first week in August.

My first impression of Nora was that she was bright, attractive and somewhat innocent. She was 30 years-old, Caucasian and well dressed. She worked as an employment recruiter in a small firm of women who filled positions for the advertising industry.

Nora began to tell me why she was coming to treatment. She stated that about 1½ years ago she began to experience a burning in her eyes and vagina along with the constant sensation that she had to urinate. She stated that these symptoms emerged immediately following an event related to a tampon. One day, she went to change her tampon and noticed that the string was gone. She tried to find it but was unsuccessful. She started to get anxious and somewhat frantic as she unsuccessfully attempted to remove it. Her anxiety grew and she reported that she was shaking, sweating, and struggling to get the tampon out. After 30 minutes she was in tears lying on the floor of the bathroom when her husband found her and brought her to the hospital. In examination at the ER they did not find anything inside her. Nora stated that she had no idea what happened to the tampon. Perhaps she took it out and didn't notice. But from that time on, she had the sensation of burning and needing to urinate.

When I asked what was happening in her life around that time, she reported that six months earlier her stepfather had died. She loved him deeply and missed him a great deal. She didn't know what he had died from; it was sudden and there was no autopsy. She also reported that a few months before her stepfather's death, she had gotten married to Jim, her current husband.

She stated that in the last 1½ years she had been to every specialist she could find to determine the causes of her somatic complaints. Each time she came up empty. No one found anything in either the eyes or the vagina to explain the sensation of burning or the need to urinate. Finally, as a last resort, her gynecologist suggested that she try psychotherapy.

I asked Nora if she had ever been in therapy. "No," she stated. "What do you imagine it will be like?" I asked. "I guess you will ask me a lot of questions and try to pull things out of me, maybe things I am not aware of." I remember hearing this and wondering if she knew what she had just said. She smiled politely and waited for my next question. I was intrigued, yet cautious, wondering how this dynamic—pulling things out of her—would play out in the transference.

In the coming weeks I began to get a picture of her current life and her early experience. The central theme that emerged in the early phase of the work was that Nora identified very strongly with the role of mediator. She would describe the way she always took care of her friends and how important it was to her that everyone stay connected. She was often aware that most people didn't put in as much effort as she did in maintaining friendships, and she had trouble understanding why. She would often have to go to great lengths to keep everyone happy and in touch. This was especially true of her family. As I heard these stories it was clear that Nora derived great meaning from this role but it also seemed to be a tremendous burden on her. She told related stories of her childhood and the circumstances after the divorce. Her father had an affair and the divorce was messy. She remembered scenes of verbal fights on the lawn, going to his house but hating it, how her mother spoke horribly of the father and how she had learned to hate him as well. She described how she was the one that had to be the mouthpiece for the mother in speaking to the father.

In this early work I stayed very close to her experience and attempted to communicate how I understood that experience. But as I would attempt to empathize with what I imagined it was like for her when people disappointed her, when she lost her father, when she was put in the middle, or when she was always being the one to reach out, she would deny any disappointment, feelings of pain, loss, or grief. She would say instead that she just wanted everyone to be happy and that she was glad to help people out. If I said, "it sounds as if you take on a great deal of burden," she would deny it. If I said, "I wonder if maybe it is disappointing that people don't put in the same effort as you," she would deny it. If I said, "was it painful to be put in the middle between your parents?" She would say, "no, it worked out alright". During this initial phase I worked very slowly and delicately as I attempted to empathize with what were clearly unacceptable feelings all the while honoring her defenses and sense of self. I persevered in my empathic interpretations and slowly she began to acknowledge that maybe everything wasn't so perfect.

My initial understanding of Nora was that she had gone through some very traumatic experiences, at this point I knew of the divorce, and that the feelings of loss, sadness, and pain appeared split off. It also seemed as if she had developed a way of surviving the situation by sacrificing her needs and feelings for the needs of others. It was my hypothesis that she was afraid of losing her mother and had to make sure that the mother was well cared for, even if it meant ignoring her own needs. In this way, it appeared as if there were two different aspects to her personality. There was the Nora that she presented to the world, a good friend, a mediator, the one without needs and without disappointment, and a second Nora, unacknowledged, the one who seemed to carry all the unwanted feelings and the one who suffered through all the disappointment. Also of importance in this split was the vilification of the father and the distance at which she kept this father, both in real life and as an internal object. She told me how difficult it was to have him at her wedding. She said, "Everyone hated him, including his own family. It was as if there was a white line down the middle of the church with him on one side and everyone else on the other side." This image of the white line splitting the father off from everything else became a meaningful metaphor to me of the state of her inner world.

One afternoon she began to talk about her stepfather who died. She described how gentle he was and how he loved women. She told me how she missed him and how she hadn't ever talked to anyone about his death. It came so sudden for her and the family generally didn't talk about things like that. As she began to speak of the loss, I became aware that I was deeply moved by her sadness. My heart felt tight and I allowed myself to be with this feeling. I realized that I was thinking of the death of my father. As I listened to her tell the story of being called suddenly to the hospital, I remembered similar events in my own life. I listened to her story of not being able to tell him what she so longed for him to hear. I told her that I knew how painful it was to lose a father. She sobbed for him and for herself. Later she told me how cleansing it felt. She told me, "I have never done that in front of anyone." I acknowledged how positive it was that she could trust me enough to let herself feel these things in my presence.

Some weeks after this she came to a session and said, "I had a dream; I want to tell you."

(Please do.)

"In the dream, my assistant at work, Janie, wanted me to go shopping with her in the city. Old Navy and Kmart. She wanted to go on Saturday. She wanted my help picking out some clothes. I am then on my way to meet her when Sue, my sister calls. She wants me to take the train with her to her home. I am alone in a café waiting to meet Janie but then decide to leave so I can make the train back with Sue. The train takes us to where Sue lives, so I am unable to meet Janie."

(What do you think about it?)

"I don't know."

(Can you tell me a little about Janie?)

"She is dating a man in the marine corps. She doesn't have very good luck with men. She was married and had a baby. Her husband was mentally abusive to her and she left. This one isn't much better. She is always upset. I try to help her but she won't let me. She never listens; she has this fantasy view of things. She is digging herself into a rut. She acts like she deserves this kind of stuff. She needs guidance but she never listens. I tried to get her to leave this guy but she won't."

(And Sue?)

"She is very different. She and I are very much alike. She has four kids and they are a very close family. I wish I was with them more. We understand each other. Both sensitive. We both love shopping. Her husband is the best. They are fun together. No fighting. Fun."

(Tell me a little about shopping with Janie)

"I love to shop. Even if it is just something small. I have never actually gone with Janie shopping."

(And Kmart and Old Navy?)

"I don't go to Old Navy or Kmart. Those places are for cheap clothes. I like better quality."

(Tell me a little about what clothes mean to you.)

"Clothes are important to me. They are how I see myself."

In exploring the dream we stayed with the idea that these two women were very different from each other. Janie is not as smart, nor as sophisticated. She has a negative view of herself and doesn't believe she deserves much. She is involved with men who treat her badly. Sue has the perfect husband and a fun life.

(So, Janie needs help and guidance and she comes to you.)

"Yes, in the dream she wants me to help her, but in real life she won't listen to me."

(Janie then, is someone who needs help but can't receive it. Why is that?)

"I don't know. I want to help her."

(It sounds like Janie is very different from you and Sue.)

"Yes."

(Is she like you in any way?)

"Janie? I don't know. Brad isn't mean to me. We don't have that kind of a life."

(I wonder if the dream is trying to communicate something to us about a part of you that is maybe a little like Janie. Is there a part of you that needs help but sometimes isn't able to receive it?)

"I don't think so."

(Well, lets keep that in mind as we go along. You know, we all have parts of us that are difficult to be with, parts of us that are stubborn or sad or angry. Maybe the dream is just telling us to see if there is a part of you that needs some attention.)

With this dream came the opportunity for Nora to begin to conceive of her inner world as inhabited by different parts, sometimes foreign to her ego and persona. The important thing that I think Nora began to consider was whether there was maybe a part of her that needed attention. I believe that even though she wasn't able to consciously assimilate this idea, I think it had an impact on the unconscious.

From the perspective of this essay, it was my understanding that the Purposive Self was producing an image that conveyed the inner object world, the defenses, and an indication of what was required by her conscious ego to further individuation.

In the sessions following this, I began to hold in mind the idea of these two distinct self states. One, the happy person who is the mediator, with no needs and no feelings, and a second self that is very sad, disappointed and traumatized—a part of her that needs help, is trying to reach out, but has trouble receiving that help. I found that I often switched back and forth between these two opposites. It was difficult to be with them both. I imagine this was true for Nora as well. One afternoon when I was very much aware of these two Noras I said to her

(I am sitting here and I am very much aware that there is a sad part of you that seems to be peeking out at me from behind a veil)

She looked at me and didn't reply.

(Does that make sense to you in any way?)

"Yes, and it feels like it's coming to the surface."

During the weeks that followed, I persevered in offering empathic interventions to what I imagined it must have been like for her going through the experiences that she reported, often without affect, with Nora smiling as she told me that her father didn't want her around, and that her mother was so angry at him that she often used Nora to tell him things related to the divorce or custody. More and more, she was able to receive my empathy and be with the feelings. I think she began to appreciate the feeling of being understood and emotionally held.

One of the layers that was uncovered around this time was related to her mother's inability to tolerate and mediate Nora's affective experience. Not only did it become clear that her mother could not tolerate the existence of any positive feeling within Nora toward the father, but she also could not tolerate any feelings of disappointment within Nora about their life after the divorce. These unwanted feelings, Nora gradually told me, had to remain hidden and virtually unknown. During this time Nora reported a dream.

"I had a weird dream. I am in the apartment of a woman, Florence, who I once worked with. Me and some other people were coming over for appetizers. I needed to shower and change and she let me use her bathroom. My mom was there with some other people and they were sitting on the bed eating. I was then also sitting on the bed. Then there were bugs, round black bugs on the window and then on my pillow. Then one got in my ear. My mom pulled it out. I remember the colors of the apartment, cream and light green. I like this color but I can't remember its name. I remember I liked the colors"

(What comes to mind about the bugs?)

"Number one, I hate bugs. I am always looking for bugs. I don't want to get close to them. For instance, the other night I saw a bug on the ceiling in our bedroom. That might have been the night I had the dream. I wonder why they could fly and why in my ear."

(Tell me about Florence?)

"She is a tough cookie. 60 years old. She loved me. I paid a lot of attention to her. She never married.

(You cared for her)

"Yeah. She is a great person, but she has a shell."

(What is that about?)

"Protection. No one ever gets too close. She pops up every once in a while."

(Anything coming to mind?)

"The bugs were oval and they could fly."

(And what about that?)

"Then they can get you. You can't know where they are going. I would love to know what it means."

(And tell me some more about Florence.)

"We both are strong and independent. We both give advice. We shared an office for awhile."

(So you were very involved?)

"She is like my mother. She doesn't like to shop. Both she and my mother are frugal. Florence is older than my mom. She needs more attention than my mom. She likes you to make a big deal about her."

(What are your feelings for Florence?)

"I liked her. You have to get to know her.

(Tell me a little about the apartment and the colors. The harmonious colors.)

"It was well done. Well put together."

(Had you ever been to her apartment in actuality?)

"No.

(What do you think about the food?)

"Apps. Appetizers. Something you have before dinner."

(What was the feeling in the dream?)

"I was freaked about the bugs. Icky."

(What do you think about the fact that you changed clothes there and showered?)

"Clothes are important to me. Like I would never wear sneakers and jeans out of the house. I want to look nice."

(So clothes are an important part of who you are?)

"Yes."

(And what do you think about the bug in your ear?)

"I was like, get it out! Where did it come from?!"

(In the dream, from the window?)

"Yea.

(Does anything come to mind with your mother pulling this out of your ear?)

"I call her for everything."

(...to get this thing out of you...)

"It was an icky thing!"

(...getting things out...)

Pause

"I guess I am becoming aware of what is bugging me. Buggy things."

(I guess I am struck by the image of pulling something out of you and how something unpleasant is being pulled out."

"My mother would never do that when I was young. I wanted people to drag things out of me. Like in High School. I wouldn't divulge what boy I liked."

(So you would keep *positive* feelings inside.)

"Yeah. I couldn't ever say anything even remotely positive about my father."

(You mean to your mother? You haven't talked about any positive feelings with your father.)

"Oh, yeah, before the divorce, we had some good times. I loved him a lot."

(Really? But there wasn't any room for those feelings, your mother couldn't receive them.)

"She was just overwhelmed. She was doing the best she could."

(No, I know, but that must have been hard for you. And it certainly adds a new layer to how you experienced the divorce.)

"I guess so."

(It is interesting where the discussion went. I am still not sure how this relates to the dream. Maybe we can explore it more next week.)

Our work with this dream during this session was both very meaningful and unclear. When I contemplated Nora's associations and her moving toward the positive feelings for her father and the boys in high school I was very much aware of the paradox in the dream. As I said to Nora, I wasn't sure what was being pulled out of her in the dream and why.

At a later point during supervision of this case, Dr. Jeffery Rubin Morey, a New York Jungian Analyst, suggested that the image of the bug in the ear could be related to the transference. He explored with me the idea that the ear is where we hear things and so perhaps the image of the bug represents some verbal intervention that was experienced as unpleasant. The mother pulling out the bug would then illustrate the defense against receiving the intervention. This would be similar to the notion of planting a bug in someone's ear.

A second amplification that came from supervision with Dr. Morey was the similarity of this image to the numerous religious depictions of the Annunciation. In these representations Mary is told by the angel Gabriel that she is to be visited and will become the virgin mother for the Christ child. In many of these depictions the words of the angel are seen as an orb traveling toward Mary's ear or as a strip of words that move toward the ear. In most of the depictions Mary is frightened by this information and is moving away from the angel. The significance of a dream image announcing a birth will take on greater significance later in the treatment.

On a more concrete level, the image of the bug and the removal would also provide a link to understanding the fact that for the first time she acknowledged that she had positive feelings for the father and that through the divorce and the vilification of the father by the mother, these feelings of loss were kept inside. The mother removing the bug I planted was the defense against the recognition of the feelings of loss.

In the next weeks I attempted to return to the dream as these themes reappeared in our work. Gradually, Nora came to recognize that she had a tremendous amount of disappointment and sadness that were buried after the divorce. She got in touch with these feelings and grew more able to tolerate their existence without resorting to denial or dissociation. This process also revealed that after the divorce, both the mother and the father used Nora to retaliate against the other. I began to understand that their rage was internalized by Nora with no hope of metabolizing it.

The work continued along these lines until one day, following a holiday break, Nora returned somewhat agitated and told me she had had a series of "baby dreams". The disturbing element in each of these dreams was that she never remembered the actual birth. The dreams were vague and didn't avail themselves much to exploration. She was agitated and anxious and then near the end of the session told me that she and her husband were trying to have a baby but that her cycle was irregular and it wasn't working. She began to cry.

(You haven't really talked at all about having a baby. Can you tell me a little about what it means to you?)

"It means everything. Having a family. Like getting married. I feel like I completed a circle when I did that. This is another circle. It makes me happy to think about it. It's about love and nurturing. I want to give a child everything my mom gave me. We always wanted it, but now we really want to try."

(I can see it is very meaningful. I am particularly struck by the idea of the circle. Like a completion.)

"Yes."

(And how does it feel to be having difficulties getting pregnant?)

"Frustrating. I'm not regular. I feel out of control. All these things that control me."

(You feel you don't have any control.)

[Pause.]

"My eyes hurt less"

(Really, what do you think about that?)

"I don't know, are they related?"

(I don't yet know. But I wonder if the feeling of lack of control brings you back to what it must have been like for you as a child. Maybe that is one of the meanings of these dreams. Perhaps they represent a part of you that is needing re-parenting. Some part of you is being born and you are experiencing that as a circle, as a completed circle. Like wholeness. I think maybe that is something that is emerging out of your work here.)

"But then why in the dream don't I remember the birth?"

(I'm not sure. Maybe we can think more about that.)

As we contemplated the meaning of forgetting the birth it always returned to the same idea.

"I don't like pain. Maybe that is why I forget."

(Is there something about our work that is painful and you want to forget?)

"No I don't think so."

(Well if there is, let me know. I think it would be important to talk about.)

With the emergence of the baby dreams and her associations of completion, circles, and fulfillment, it was my sense that the psyche was producing symbols of wholeness and specifically a symbol of a new self being born. Maybe then the bug in the ear dream was in some way an announcement of the beginning of individuation. Through the process of treatment we had reestablished a connection to the inner developmental processes and the symbol of a new child represented the new psychic organization that was being born. This follows directly from the Jungian perspective and within that model these dreams as they appeared within the context of the treatment would represent the beginning of individuation.

In addition to the symbolic level of the birth, there was also the literal level. Nora and her husband were trying to conceive a child and were having difficulties. The dreams could represent an anxiety response to this difficult and disappointing process. My sense was that both these levels, the literal and the symbolic, needed to be held.

The next week Nora began by telling me that there was something that she remembered after last week's session.

"I don't know how I didn't connect it. I just forgot about it. Probably because I blocked it."

(Tell me.)

"When I was twenty I had an abortion. I was with a stupid boy friend who I didn't like very much. There was no way I could have had the baby. I just can't help wondering…am I being punished for that? Is that why I can't get pregnant? Like I had my chance. I mean, I couldn't have taken care of it. I remembered after last week. Not a lot of people know, my two roommates at that time from college. Jim knows."

(And your mother?)

"No. I couldn't ever imagine telling her. Or my sisters."

(Do you want to talk about it?)

She did, tentatively at first and then in more detail. We also talked about why it was so hard for her to tell her family. They would have been disappointed and unable to help. She spoke a great deal about feeling punished, like she had done something wrong. It was very hard for me to sit with her feelings of self-punishment. I noticed moments where I imagined interrupting her and interjecting some benign platitude. I realized that the despair I was witnessing was very similar to the feelings I had as a child when I was alone with overwhelming experience. I realized that this was the challenge, to be able to receive this pain, to not try to make it go away, but instead, to just be with it. At one point she put her hand to her chest. It seemed like the feeling was stuck there.

(What are you feeling under your hand?)

"Pressure...I need to please...I feel I will let her down...I don't want her to be disappointed...Oh, my God...I can't deal with this...I'm never going to please her"

[Sobbing]

[long pause.]

(What will happen if you don't?)

"She will be disappointed."

[Crying—pause]

"I was too alone"

(You couldn't risk losing her, all of these experiences as a child and young woman...you had to go through it all alone. It is very sad.)

We talked more about the abortion. I wasn't sure if I should draw a connection to the tampon removal experience. It seemed linked, but I decided to wait. We also talked about the idea of being punished. She spoke of how God was disappointed with her and punishing her. She called it a black cloud over her. I told her that I believed that God had only compassion for her, a young woman who had no one to turn to and who was unable to get help from her mother. I told her that her decision was very difficult. I also told how important I thought it was that given the experiences with her mother that she could trust me enough to work through this.

Several threads all seemed to come together with this session. There was her feeling that something inside her needed to come out. The abortion was very difficult for her with regards to this because she longed for a child but it was the wrong time and the wrong father. In this way, something she viewed as wonderful became something unwanted and something that had to be removed. The complexity of this issue and her guilt over making this difficult decision infused the idea of something being inside her with great meaning. In terms of the transference, these themes took on even greater significance. Her original idea of therapy was that I would ask her questions and pull things out of her. Taken in the context of the present discussion, then, I am either to be an obstetrician or an abortionist. I imagined also, that her desire to have me take responsibility for pulling things out of her was a way to avoid taking full responsibility for her choice and what she needed to do in relation to her pregnancy. I think it also represented to her a clear demonstration that I was interested enough in her to desire what was inside.

In the next session we returned to the abortion and Nora continued to work through and grieve her loss. I then made the link between the abortion and the tampon and together we wondered whether they were related. Blood was the image that brought them together for Nora. She didn't like blood and she didn't like menstruation. This led her to tell me about when her cycle began.

"I was twelve or thirteen. My mom wasn't home. I had to tell my father. He said, 'congrats, you're a woman'. I was embarrassed and when my mom came home she made me call the swim coach and tell him why I couldn't make practice that day."

(That must have been hard for you?)

"I guess. And now I am very fussy about my tampon. I change it a lot."

(Why is that?)

"I feel dirty otherwise. It's a clean thing. I think that is why it was so awful that day when I couldn't get the tampon out."

Immediately following this session there was a change. Nora came in beaming and told me she thought she was pregnant. "Maybe the black cloud has lifted." A week later it was confirmed; Nora was pregnant. My experience of her after this was that she was somehow lighter and not as tightly held. She was clearly ecstatic and for a few weeks we explored the feelings of joy and what it meant to have the black cloud lifted. She reported that her eyes and vagina were not burning, that she hadn't been thinking about them.

My approach to the idea of birth was to always maintain a bifocal view of it. I held to the idea that the birth was taking place on two levels: the literal and the psychological. The work continued uninterrupted for a number of weeks until we neared the time when I would need to let her know that I would be leaving the clinic and unable to continue with her. I allowed 8 weeks for the termination, but was still concerned about the potential impact especially given her experience with failing caregivers. Nora received the news and didn't bat an eye. I told her that many different kinds of feelings might come up at a time like this and that I thought it would be good to discuss all of them. A week later she brought in a dream.

"I was driving with my mom down a hill toward the house I grew up in. We were going to pick up my dad. We stop and he gets in. Next, I am at the hospital waiting to go into the delivery room to have a baby. I am sitting in the waiting room next to my mom with my head on her shoulder. Next, I had the baby but I couldn't remember anything about the birth. My mom showed me the baby in the nursery and it was premature. I thought, why can't I remember. Next, I am out of the hospital in a car going to pick up my dad. We get him and head up the hill toward the hospital, we are going to the hospital to see the baby."

(What was the feeling in the dream?)

"Bizarre. Why my dad? Why not my husband?

(Any thoughts about not remembering the birth?)

"Weird. What am I nervous about? What am I trying to block out? Pain. I know I don't deal with pain well. This is another dream where I don't remember."

(So, something you don't want to remember related to pain?)

"What do you think?"

(I think you are expressing it well. Symbolically, something you are giving birth to, and we have discussed how that might be related to your process here, that you are wanting to remain unconscious of.)

"The process. My dad...why would I want him there."

(Perhaps that is the important difference that the dream is showing. He is *with* you and not on the other side of the white line. I wonder if it is talking about a union within you that is bringing forth some new part of you, some new aspect of your self.)

"Yeah, cause I don't think in real life they would both be there."

(Right, so it is more symbolic. Maybe more about the inner birth.)

Nora then told a story of how she wanted to visit her father and how the mother prevented her from doing so. She also related a story of the grandmother sitting Nora down after the divorce and detailing the crimes of the father. We then returned to the dream.

(Do you have any thoughts about the baby being premature?)

"I don't know. I worry about things like that. What if that happens?"

(And what would it mean symbolically, do you think, in relation to what is being born through your therapy?)

"I don't know. What do you mean?"

(I am not sure. Maybe we can explore a little bit about what you might imagine is being born here, symbolically. What will this child be like?)

"It will have confidence, strength, power. I see a little face, adorable. Eyes wide open. Ready to take on the world."

(And what do you think is painful about this process here that you might not want to remember?)

"Feelings, painful feelings. When we hit a nerve. Tender spots. Stuff with my mother and father. [Pause] Is this a way I keep a mask on and don't see the real me?"

(What do you mean?)

"Like behind the veil. [pause] When they first got separated and we didn't want to talk to him it was so awful. I missed him. I loved him a lot."

(This is something you haven't talked about much.)

"No, I just blocked it all out. It was just...one day he was bad."

(In that sense it is not remembered. If he is just bad then there is no loss, no pain, right?)

"But where do the feelings go?"

(That's a good question. I think maybe the dream is addressing that.)

We were just about out of time so we picked up the discussion of the dream the following week. Nora began.

"I have been thinking about it. What does it all mean?"

(Let's talk a little more about the idea of the premature birth. Anything come to mind?)

"Premature. The baby stays in the hospital. It isn't yet ready to leave."
(Right. You know, I was wondering about the idea of the premature birth and whether that might have some connection to our ending.)

"In what way?"

(In the sense that maybe it is happening a little too soon.)

"I don't feel bad about it. Maybe the ending will be fine. Maybe it means that I need to take over for myself now. Maybe I need to do the work now."

(Okay, that may be true. I think you will be fine, but if you had a premature baby, what would you do?)

"I don't know. You mean like for food and warmth, so it can thrive?"

(Right. I think one of the things is monitoring it for food and warmth. To make sure it can thrive, as you say. Does that make any sense to you?)

"Monitoring it."

(Yeah. And maybe think a little more about whether you want to continue therapy with someone after me. I will be happy to give you a referral if you want one.)

"Okay."

My understanding of the dream follows the basic formulation already outlined. I think the dream was telling us that the termination was happening a little bit too soon. Not that the baby was in danger, but that it needed some extra attention and care. But impacting this is the other aspect of the dream, the forgetting. And it is this aspect that might adversely determine how well Nora can care for what has been generated in the therapy. It was my hypothesis, supported I believe by the dream, that the more Nora could remain conscious of the process, including the pain of the loss, the more our termination could become a repair and not a re-wounding.

In the coming weeks I worked with Nora to help her remain conscious of the difficult feelings that were underneath the termination process. She was able to get close to feelings of disappointment by using the somatic level. She told me that her eyes still burned sometimes. I acknowledged that we weren't able to fully complete that work. She also told me that if she started with another therapist that she would want someone in private practice. I acknowledged that she was aware that I had limitations in my ability to meet her needs. I was supportive of the fact that she wanted to get the best possible care. But also important in these last sessions was the awareness of the deep connection that we shared. Much as she wanted to appear like the end of our work didn't matter, I knew better. This was the father transference. I was leaving and she would tell herself that I wasn't so special after all. No reason to feel bad. We were then up to the final session.

"I had another one of those dreams. I don't remember much. I remember walking down the street where I grew up. I went to a friend's house. We are still friends now, we talk a lot. I rang her doorbell. She says, what are you doing here, you just had a baby. Then she calls my mom and sisters. Then she takes me down the block to my house from childhood. Then I was inside with my sisters and Jim and my sister's husband. We are in a circle. My one sister tells the story of the birth. She said, you went into labor, it was painful. Then I woke up."

(What was the feeling?)

"Confusion."

(Can you say more?)

"I was confused when she was confused."

(So it is the same theme.)

"There is no child, the process is missing. I am scared of the process. Of it hurting."

(Do you mean in terms of your actual pregnancy?)

"Yeah. If it hurts."

(That is very understandable. How would this relate to the symbolic level and our work here and what has been born in you?)

"It is definitely related to childhood. Where I grew up."

(Would you think it is related to our ending?)

"I don't know. I know you keep talking about that, but I think you did a really good job."

(What will it be like next week when you don't come here?)

"Two things. Free. And also…it's good to unload."

(You'll miss unloading…[Pause.] Is there any feelings or thoughts coming up now?)

"Vulnerable, I guess."

(Vulnerable, to what?)

[Pause.]

123

"These memories of endings are coming, of being disappointed. I remember once in Junior high school when I wanted to be friends with this girl and she wrote a note to another girl and I read it. It was very mean. I was excluded. I really liked her."

(It is very hard to feel left out. [Pause] Do you experience these feelings in your body anywhere?)

"My chest"

(Go into that feeling, if you can. Breathe into it.) [Pause]

"I feel the sadness.

[Pause. Crying.]

I suppose I don't want to remember the pain. Is that bad?"

(It makes perfect sense.)

"I'm going to miss you."

(I know. It is so good that you can be with these feeling and not block them out. [Pause] What might also be important to remember is that the dream is telling us that even though you may sometimes want to block things out, that there is a part of you that remembers the whole thing. In the dream your sister tells you. There is the circle. Like today, you were able to get in touch with the feelings of connection and the loss.)

"I will miss this work."

(And I will miss you. It has meant a great deal to me to work with you.)

"Thank you."

(You're welcome. And I have that referral for you.)

Summary

In this treatment my goal was to use Jungian ideas related to the Purposive Self in conjunction with contemporary ideas from psychoanalysis and developmental theory. Formulating an initial picture of the inner world of the patient was arrived at through an understanding of her early experience—internalization of objects, self experience, and defensive organization—as well as an appreciation for the unfolding of individuation that evolved through the dreams emerging during treatment. The Self of the patient was understood as the organizing construct around which my interventions were organized. Not only was I attempting to understand and empathize with traumatic experience, coping strategies, and defenses, but I was also using the dreams to help me in understanding the ways in which the Self needed to change.

The primary stance I took in relation to her experience was empathic. I acknowledged what she was consciously aware of and also extended my empathy to a layer just beneath the surface to a place where Nora had difficulty navigating. In this way I attempted to facilitate her approach to these areas of her inner world that were painful and highly defended. At each step, I had to strike a delicate balance between honoring her defenses and helping her to expand her consciousness. It was my intention to support and contain her sufficiently so she could feel safe enough to do this work.

Nora's dreams offered a clear view of the inner world and the process of individuation as our work unfolded. In the first dream we saw the ambivalence of the ego in relation to the process of caring for the parts of her that needed help. The second dream of the bugs in the ear carried many meanings related to what was inside her, how it got there, and her anxiety about getting it out. The dream had a level of meaning that resonated with the transference and the ways in which she tended to reject what I offered. It also had reverberations to the ways in which her feelings about her father were trapped inside her and plucked out by the mother. Finally, the baby dreams chart the course of her developing Self through treatment. Again, her difficulty was staying with the process and the potential pain of the process. The last two dreams in the series offered an opportunity to make adjustments in the work to better care for the needs of the Self. With the announcement of termination, Nora fell back into the pattern of defense that she developed in childhood when confronted with loss: don't let yourself feel, you have to take care of yourself. It was very difficult for her to get in touch with the pain connected with the ending. The dreams in this last stage helped a great deal in understanding these dynamics and in developing an approach to help her ameliorate this experience.

Chapter Seven: Conclusion

Two areas of psychoanalytic theory, the self and the dream, have been reviewed to facilitate an understanding of the ameliorative tendencies inherent in the psyche. Together, these two areas map out the terrain whereby the Purposive Self might become identifiable both from its context in an underlying model of the mind, and from the manifestation of the purposive through dreaming. What has emerged from this review is a complex picture whereby one both finds a great deal of psychoanalytic theory that approaches these purposive processes and simultaneously, a great deal of tension which appears to move theorists away from a full explication of these tendencies.

In studying the construct of the self, three distinct domains of human experience were identified as being formulated in the various conceptualizations appearing in the work of theorists as the construct evolved and changed. This evolution began with Freud's *das ich* (1915, 1923) and developed through Hartmann's expansion of the ego (1939, 1948, 1950, 1956), Sullivan's relational emphasis (1940), Winnicott's True and False Selves, Kohut's self psychology (1971, 1977, 1984), and Bromberg's multiplicity of self (1991, 1993, 1996). Several trends and changes in understanding the nature of the self emerged in this review. First, there was an increasing emphasis on the importance of relational dynamics in an understanding of the formation and development of the self. Second, the dismantling of Freud's metapsychology and the movement toward postmodernism necessitated several important alterations in conceptualizations of the self in the domains of the *Self as Person*, the *Self as Core*, and the *Self as Process*. And third, recent theory and research on the development of the self in infancy has served to replace the loss of this classical metapsychology.

Within the domain of the *Self as Person*, the notion of unity of self became highly contentious. Building on Sullivan's illusion of self, Bromberg convincingly illustrated the importance and relevance of conceptualizing the self as a relationally determined phenomenon and not a static unity. Related to this shift was the growing difficulty with the concept of the *Self as Core* when conceived as something invariant, inherited, true, or authentic. These conceptualizations, according to certain theorists (Sullivan, 1940; Khan,

1974; Bromberg, 1991, 1993) were built upon the unsupportable biological bases of the Freudian metapsychology or were dangerously close to the religious concept of the soul. What has replaced these unsupported notions are models of the *Self as Core* that emerge out of infant developmental theory (Emde, 1983) and neurobiological research (Schore, 1994, 1997). These more recent conceptualizations form a model whereby the *Self as Core* is relationally determined and internalized through the process of dyadic affect regulation with the primary caregiver.

Imbedded in these recent notions of the *Self as Core* and the *Self as Person* are the changing ideas related to the *Self as Process*. Once the foundation for a unified self was destabilized through the growing dissatisfaction with Freud's metapsychology and the infusion of postmodernism, there was no longer a logical necessity to have a process of maintaining cohesion. What was once thought to be a central characteristic in several major models of the self (Hartmann, 1956; Winnicott, 1949, 1962; Kohut, 1971, 1977; Lachmann, 1996) became an unsupportable relic of drives and Freudian metapsychology. Along with the lost concept of cohesion, however, came several other losses related to the *Self as Process*. These lost concepts of process relate to understandings of primary creativity, original thought, and the function, formation, and meaning of dreams. It is this loss of conceptual and clinical power that this essay has addressed.

The review of the clinical use of dreams and underlying dream theory presented in this essay provides a glimpse into the growing separation of dream interpretation from dream theory. In Freud's original model, dream interpretation was directly dependent upon the underlying model of dream function and formation: the preservation of sleep/discharge/disguise/wish fulfillment model. In this model, there is an idea with a charge attached, a sexual wish, that is pressing for release. The censor, however, hoping to preserve sleep, is unwilling to allow this wish to be experienced by the ego. Through the dream work, then, the censor disguises the latent content, the sexual wish, as the manifest dream. From there, dream interpretation involves a process of arriving at the underlying latent content through free association from the elements of the manifest content; the manifest content itself has no direct relationship to the true meaning of the dream. In this model there was a perfect harmony between the interpretive perspective, the model of dream function, and the model of the mind.

From these earliest conceptions of the dream there was a steady shift, already in play in the work of Freud, toward a greater acceptance of the manifest content as a meaningful unit of communication. Exceptions to the wish fulfillment model, the punishment dream and the trauma dream, revealed areas where Freud's theory was weak and slowly clinicians began to use the dream differently. As was evidenced in the review of the use of dreams, there were several key factors in clinical theory that accompanied this phenomenon. These included changes in technique, changes in the model of the mind, and changes in the view of the unconscious. The result of these changes was that, increasingly, dream interpretation became more and more detached from an underlying model able to account for why and how the dream was being produced. The importance of this shift lies in the inability to explain the existence of a meaningful communication, the manifest dream, emerging from the psyche. Without Freud's mechanisms for the dreamwork, disguise and deception, there was no structure, no process within psychoanalytic theory to explain what produces the dream and for what purpose.

Following the general thesis of this essay, then, these two areas, the self and the dream, reveal an aspect of the human experience that is undeveloped in psychoanalytic theory: the Purposive Self. Jungian concepts and theory for the Self as purposive have been introduced as a way to build a model of the mind and a model of treatment capable of integrating the construct of a Purposive Self into a contemporary psychodynamic model of treatment.

The Jungian Self is a center of the personality, situated within the unconscious, which parallels the position of the ego within consciousness. The Self, however, is understood to be the source and center of the entire psyche, ego included. This prominence of the Self supports the Jungian view that individuation, the process of becoming oneself, involves a recognition of, and negotiation with, this internal source and guide. Individuation is a dialogue between the ego and the Self where opposites are held and new potentials emerge. Dreams are the language of this unconscious Self and when recognized as meaningful, they can offer guidance, reveal the inner world, and further the development of personality. As Jung (1944) states

We know that the mask of the unconscious is not rigid—it reflects the face we turn towards it. (p. 29)

Bibiography

Abraham, H. C. & Freud, E. L. (1965). The Freud-Abraham letters, 1907-26.

Arlow, J. & Brenner, C. (1964). Dreams and the Structural Theory. In Psychoanalytic concepts and the structural theory.

Bacal, H. & Newman, K. (1990). Theories of object relations: bridges to self psychology. New York: Columbia University Press.

Beebe, J; Cambray, J.; & Kirsch, T. (2001). What Freudians Can Learn From Jung. Psychoanalytic Psychology, 18 (2) 213-242.

Bion, W. R. (1959). Attacks on Linking. International Journal of Psycho-Analysis, 40, 308-315.

Bion, W.R. (1977). Beyond memory and desire. International journal of psychoanalysis.

Blumenberg (1983). Legitimacy of the modern age. Boston: MIT Press.

Bollas, C. (1987). The shadow of the object: Psychoanalysis of the unthought known. New York: Columbia University Press.

Bonine, W. (1964) The Role of dreams in psychoanalysis. In J. Masserman, Ed. Science and psychoanalysis, volume 17. New York: Grune and Stratton.

Brenner (1969, 1992). Dreams in clinical psychoanalytic practice. In Essential papers on dreams. (1992). New York: New York University Press.

Bromberg, P. (1991). On knowing one's patient inside out: The aesthetics of unconscious communication. Psychoanalytic Dialogues, 1 (4), 399-422.

Bromberg, P. (1993). Shadow and substance: A relational perspective on clinical process. Psychoanalytic Psychology, 10 (2), 147-168.

Bromberg (1996). Standing in the spaces. Contemporary Psychoanalysis, 32 (4), 509-535.

Charet, F.X. (1993). Spiritualism and the foundations of C.G. Jung's psychology. Albany, NY: SUNY Press.

Charet, F.X. (2000). Understanding Jung: recent biographies and scholarship. The Journal of Analytical Psychology, 45, 195-216.

Chomsky, N. (1968). Language and the mind. Psychology Today, 1 (9), 48-51, 66-68.

Curtis, H. & Sachs, D. (1976). Dialogue on the changing use of the dream in psychoanalytic practice. International Journal of Psychoanalysis, 57, 343-354.

Diamond, S.; Balvin, R. S.; Diamond, F. R. (1963). Inhibition and choice. Oxford: Harper & Row.

Edinger, E. (1984). The Creation of consciousness: Jung's myth for modern man. Toronto: Inner City Books.

Eigen, M. (1981). The area of faith in Winnicott, Lacan, and Bion. International Journal of Psychoanalysis, 62, 413-433.

Ellenberger, H. (1970). The Discovery of the unconscious. New York: Basic Books.

Emde, R. (1983). The prerepresentational self and its affective core. Psychoanalytic Study of the Child. 38, 165-192.

Erickson, E. (1963). Childhood and society. New York: Norton.

Fairbairn, (1952). Psychoanalytic study of the personality. Oxford, England: Routledge.

Fairbairn, W.R.D. (1931). Features in the Analysis of a Patient with a physical Genital Abnormality. In Psychoanalytic studies of the personality. Oxford, England: Routledge.

Fairbairn, W.R.D. (1944, 1952). Endopsychic Structure Considered in Terms of Object Relationships. In Psychoanalytic study of the personality (1952) Oxford, England: Routledge.

Ferenczi, S. (1934). On the revision of the interpretation of dreams. Indian Journal of Psychology, 9, 1-2 34-38.

Ferenczi S. (1922). Psychoanalysis and the war neuroses. New York: Stechert.

Fordham, M. (1984). Review of Meltzer's Dream Life. In Freud, Jung, Klein: The fenceless field. (1995) New York: Routledge.

Fordham, M. (1995). Freud, Jung, and Klein: The fenceless field. New York: Routledge.

Fosha, D. (2000). The Transforming power of affect. New York: Basic Books.

Fosshage, J. (1983). The Psychological Function of Dreams: A revised Psychoanalytic Perspective. In M. Lansky, Ed. Essential papers on dreams. (1992) New York: New York University Press.

Fosshage, J. (1997). The organizing functions of dream mentation. Contemporary Psychoanalysis, 33 (3), 429-458.

Fosshage, J. (2000). The organizing functions of dreaming—A contemporary psychoanalytic model: Commentary on paper by Hazel Ipp. Psychoanalytic Dialogues, 10 (1), 103-117.

Frederickson (2000). There's something "youey" about you: The polyphonic unity of personhood. Contemporary Psychoanalysis, 36 (4), 587-617.

Friedland, B. (1978). Toward a psychology of the self. Contemproary psychoanalysis, 10, 346-357.

Friedman, M. (1957). Representative and Typical Dreams With Emphasis on the Masculinity Femininity Problem. The Psychoanalytic Review, 44 (4), 363-389.

Freud, S. (1900). The Interpretation of Dreams. Standard Edition IV and V. London: Hogarth Press.

Freud (1901). Fragment of an analysis of a case of hysteria. Standard Edition VII. London: Hogarth Press.

Freud, S. (1914). On the history of the psychoanalytic movement. In Standard Edition, Vol. XIV. London: Hogarth Press.

Freud, (1915). On Narcissism. Standard Edition XIV. London: Hogarth Press.

Freud, S. (1916, 1959). The Metapsychological Supplement to the Theory of Dreams. In Collected papers. (1959) New York: Basic Books.

Freud, (1917). Introductory Lectures. In Standard Edition XVI. London: Hogarth Press.

Freud (1919). The Interpretation of Dreams. Standard Edition IV and V. London: Hogarth Press.

Freud, S. (1920). Beyond the Pleasure Principle. Standard Edition XVIII. London: Hogarth Press.

Freud, S. (1923). The Ego and the Id. Standard Edition XVIV. London: Hogarth Press.

Freud (1923b). Remarks on the theory and interpretation of dreams. Standard Edition XIX. London: Hogarth Press.

Freud, S. (1924). A short account of psychoanalysis. Standard Edition XI. London: Hogarth Press.

Freud, S. (1933, 1992). Revision of the Theory of Dreams. In M. Lansky (Ed.), Essential papers on dreams. (1992) New York: New York University Press.

Freud (1937). Analysis Terminable and Interminable. Standard Edition XXIII. London: Hogarth Press.

Freud, (1940). An Outline of Psychoanalysis. Standard Edition XXIII. London: Hogarth Press.

Fromm, E. (1950). Psychoanalysis and religion. New Haven: Yale University Press.

Fromm, E. (1951). The forgotten language: an introduction to the understanding of dreams, fairy tales and myths. Oxford, England: Rinehart.

Gallant, C. (1996). Tabooed Jung. New York: New York University Press.

Gedo, J. (1983). Portraits of the artist. Hillsdale, NJ: The Analytic Press.

Frank Faranda

Gedo, J. (1997). Reflections on metapsychology, theoretical coherence, hermeneutics, and biology. Journal of the American Psychoanalytic Association, 45 (3), 779-806

Gedo, J. (1999). Evolution of psychoanalysis: Contemporary theory and practice. New York: Other Press.

Gedo, J. (1999a) The Theory of Development and the Yield of Infant Observation. In Evolution of psychoanalysis: Contemporary theory and practice. New York: Other Press.

Gedo, J. & Goldberg, A. (1973). Models of the mind: A psychoanalytic theory. Oxford, England: University of Chicago Press.

Gershman H. (1981). Current application of Horney's theory to dream interpretation. American Journal of Psychoanalysis, 43 (3), 219-229

Greenberg, J. & Mitchell, S. (1983). Object relations in psychoanalytic theory. Cambridge, MA.: Harvard University Press.

Greenson, R. (1970). The Exceptional Position of the Dream in Psychoanalytic Practice. In M. Lansky, M., Ed., Essential papers on dreams. (1992) New York: New York University Press.

Grotstein, J. (2000). Who is the dreamer who dreams the dream. Hillsdale, NJ: The Analytic Press.

Grubrich-Simitis, I. (2000). Metamorphoses of the interpretation of dreams: Freud's conflicted relations with his book of the century. International Journal of Psychoanalysis, 81 (6), 1155-1183.

Guntrip, H. (1994). Personal relations therapy. Northvale, NJ: Jason Aronson.

Gutheil, E. (1951, 1960). The handbook of dream analysis. Oxford, England: Grove Press.

Hartmann, H. (1939). Ego psychology and the problem of adaptation. Oxford, England: International Universities Press.

Hartmann, H. (1948). Comments on the psychoanalytic theory of instinctual drives. Psychoanalytic Quarterly. 17, 368-388.

Hartmann, H. (1950). Essays on ego psychology. Oxford, England: International University Press.

Hartmann, (1956). The development of the ego concept in Freud's work. International Journal of Psycho-Analysis, 37 (6), 425-437.

Hayman, R. (2001). A life of Jung. New York: Norton.

Hoffman, I. (1992). Some practical implications of a social-constructivist view of the psychoanalytic situation. Psychoanalytic Dialogues, 2, 287-304.

Holt, R. (1989). Freud reappraised: A fresh look at psychoanalytic theory. New York: Guilford Press.

Homans, P. (1978). Jung in context. Chicago: University of Chicago Press.

Homans, P. (1989). The ability to mourn: disillusionment and the social origins of psychoanalysis. Chicago: University of Chicago Press.

Horney, K. (1950). Neurosis and human growth; the struggle toward self-realization. Oxford, England: W. W. Norton.

Jacobson, E. (1964). The self and the object world. Oxford, England: International Universities Press.

Jacoby, M. (1990). Individuation and narcissism: The psychology of Jung and Kohut. New York: Routledge.

Jacoby, M. (2000). The growing convergence of contemporary psycho-analysis and Jungian analysis. Psychoanalytic Dialogues, 10 (3), 489-503.

Jones, E. (1955). The life and work of Sigmund Freud. New York: Basic Books.

Jung, C.G. (1896-99). The Zofingia lectures. In Collected Works, supplemental volume A. Princeton, NJ: Princeton University Press.

Jung, C.G. (1905). On Spiritualistic Phenomena. In Collected Works, volume 18. Princeton, NJ: Princeton University Press.

Jung, C.G. (1907). The psychology of dementia praecox. In Collected Works, volume 3. Princeton, NJ: Princeton University Press.

Jung, C.G. (1912). The psychology of the unconscious. In Collected Works, supplemental volume B. Princeton, NJ: Princeton University Press.

Jung, C.G. (1913). Contribution to the study of psychological types. In Collected Works, volume 6. Princeton, NJ: Princeton University Press.

Jung, C.G. (1916). Adaptation, Individuation, Collectivity. In Collected Works, volume 18. Princeton, NJ: Princeton University Press.

Jung, C.G. (1916a). General aspects of dream psychology. In Collected works, volume 8. Princeton, NJ: Princeton University Press.

Jung, C.G. (1920). The psychological foundation of belief in spirits. In Collected Works, volume 8. Princeton, NJ: Princeton University Press.

Jung, C.G. (1921). Psychological types. In Collected Works, volume 6. Princeton, NJ: Princeton University Press.

Jung, C.G. (1928). The relation between the ego and the unconscious. In Collected Works, volume 7. Princeton, NJ: Princeton University Press.

Jung, C.G. (1931). The aims of psychotherapy. In Collected Works, volume 16. Princeton, NJ: Princeton University Press.

Jung, C.G. (1933). The meaning of psychology for modern man. In Collected Works, volume 10. Princeton, NJ: Princeton University Press.

Jung, C.G. (1934). Practical use of dream analysis. In Collected Works, volume 16. Princeton, NJ: Princeton University Press.

Jung C.G. (1935). Archetypes in the collective unconscious. In Collected works, volume 9. Princeton, NJ: Princeton University Press.

Jung C.G. (1936). The concept of the collective unconscious. In Collected works, volume 9. Princeton, NJ: Princeton University Press.

Jung C.G. (1939). Psychological aspects of the mother archetype. In Collected Works, volume 9. Princeton, NJ: Princeton University Press.

Jung, C.G. (1944). Psychology and alchemy. In Collected Works, volume 12. Princeton, NJ: Princeton University Press.

Jung, C.G. (1945). On the nature of dreams. In Collected Works, volume 8. Princeton, NJ: Princeton University Press.

Jung, C.G. (1947). On the nature of the psyche. In Collected Works, volume 8. Princeton, NJ: Princeton University Press.

Jung, C.G. (1948). Psychology and Religion. In Collected Works, volume 11. Princeton, NJ: Princeton University Press.

Jung, C.G. (1949). The psychology of the child archetype. In Collected Works, volume 9. Princeton, NJ: Princeton University Press.

Jung, C.G. (1951). Aion. In Collected Works, volume 9. Princeton, NJ: Princeton University Press.

Jung, C.G. (1952). Answer to Job. In <u>Collected Works, volume 11</u>. Princeton, NJ: Princeton University Press.

Jung C.G. (1954). Development of personality. In <u>Collected Works, volume 17.</u> Princeton, NJ: Princeton University Press.

Jung, C.G. (1963). <u>Memories, dreams, reflections</u>. New York: Pantheon Books.

Kahn, M. (1976). The changing use of dreams in psychoanalytic practice: In search of the dreaming experience. <u>International Journal of Psycho-Analysis, 57</u> (3), 325-330.

Kalsched, D. (2000). Jung's contribution to psychoanalytic thought. <u>Psychoanalytic Dialogues, 10</u> (3), 473-488.

Klein, G. (1976). <u>Psychoanalytic theory: An exploration of essentials.</u> New York: International University Press.

Klein, M. (1932). <u>The psycho-analysis of children.</u> New York: Norton.

Kohut, (1971). <u>The Analysis of the self</u>. Madison, WI: International University Press.

Kohut, H. (1977). <u>The Restoration of the self</u>. Madison, WI: International University Press.

Kohut, H. (1984). <u>How does analysis cure?</u> Chicago: The University of Chicago Press.

Kuras, M. (2000). Balder's bad dream: Jung's relevance to the postmodern condition. <u>Quadrant: Journal of the C. G. Jung Foundation for Analytical Psychology, 30</u> (1), 24-46.

Lachmann, F. (1996). How many selves make a person. <u>Contemporary Psychoanalysis, 32</u> (4), 595-614.

Lansky, M. (1992). The legacy of the interpretation of dreams. In M. Lansky, Ed., Essential papers on dreams. (1992) New York: New York University Press.

Lesser, R. (1978). The theory of the self in contemporary psychoanalysis. Contemporary Psychoanalysis, 14, 545-548.

Levin (1969). The self: A contribution to its place in theory and technique. International Journal of Psycho-Analysis, 50 (1), 41-51.

Lichtenstein, H. (1977). The dilemma of human identity. New York: Jason Aronson.

Lippmann, P. (2000). Dreams and Psychoanalysis: A Love—Hate Story. Psychoanalytic Psychology, 17 (4), 627-650.

Loewald, H. W. (1977). Transference and countertransference: the roots of psychoanalysis. Book review essay on the Freud Jung letters. The Psychoanalytic Quarterly, 46 (3), 514-527.

Lorand, S. (1956). The dream in the practice of psychoanalysis. Journal of the American Psychoanalytic Association, 4, 122-137.

Mahler, M.; Pine, F.; & Bergman, A. (1975). The psychological birth of the human infant. New York: Basic Books.

McGuire, Wm. (1974). The Freud/Jung letters. Princeton: Princeton University Press.

Meltzer, D. (1983). Dream-life: A reexamination of psychoanalytic theory and technique. London: Clunie.

Modell, A. H. (1976). The holding environment and the therapeutic action of psychoanalysis. Journal of the American psychoanalytic association, 24, 285-308.

Mullahy, P. (1945). A theory of interpersonal relations and the evolution of personality. <u>Psychiatry: Journal for the Study of Interpersonal Processes, 8,</u> 177-205.

Nagy, M. (1991). <u>Philosophical issues in the psychology of C.G. Jung.</u> Albany, NY: SUNY Press.

Neumann, E. (1996). <u>The Child</u>. London: Hodder & Staughton.

Newirth, J. (2001). Creating meaning: the symbolic in psychoanalytic theory. <u>Paper Delivered at Division 39 APA conference</u>, April 2001.

Nietzche (1909). <u>Beyond good and evil.</u> Collected Works, volume 12. London: Knopf.

Nunberg H. & Federn, P. <u>Minutes of the Vienna psychoanalytic society. (1962-1967). Vols. 1-2</u>. New York: International University Press.

Ogden, T. (1997). <u>Reverie and interpretation</u>. Northvale, NJ: Jason Aronson.

Ogden, T. (1986, 1997). <u>The matrix of the mind</u>. Northvale, NJ: Jason Aronson.

Padel, J. (1978). Object Relational Approach. In <u>Dream Interpretation: A Comparative Study.</u>

Palmer, M. (1997). <u>Freud and Jung on religion.</u> New York: Routledge.

Perls, F. (1949, 1967). <u>Ego, hunger, and aggression</u>. New York: Vintage Books.

Rangell, L. (1980) The self in psychoanalytic theory. <u>Journal of the American Psychoanalytic Society, 30,</u> 863-891.

Ricoeur, P. (1993). Freud & philosophy: an essay on Interpretation. New Haven, CT: Yale University Press.

Rieff, P. (1966, 1987). The Triumph of the therapeutic: uses of faith after Freud. Chicago: University of Chicago Press.

Rosenblatt and Thikstun (1970). A study of the concept of psychic energy. International Journal of Psycho-Analysis, 51 (3) 265-278.

Samuels, A. (1985). Jung and the post-Jungians. New York: Routledge.

Samuels, A. (2000). Post-Jungian dialogues. Psychoanalytic Dialogues, 10 3, 403-426.

Sandler, J. & Rosenblatt, B. (1962). The concept of the representational world. Psychoanalytic Study of the Child, 17, 128-145.

Saperstein, J. & Gaines, J. (1973). Metapsychological considerations of the self. International Journal of Psycho-Analysis, 54, 415-424.

Saul, L. (1958). Technic and practice of psychoanalysis. Philadelphia: J. B. Lippincott.

Schacht (1988). Winnicott's position in regard to the self with special reference to childhood. International Review of Psycho-Analysis, 15, 515-529.

Schaefer, R. (1976). A new language for psychoanalysis. New Haven, CT: Yale University Press.

Schafer, R. (1999). Recentering psychoanalysis. New York: Basic Books.

Schore, A. (1994). Affect regulation and the origin of the self: The neurobiology of emotional development. Hillsdale, NJ: Lawrence Erlbaum Associates.

Schore, A. (1997). A century after Freud's project: Is a rapprochement between psychoanalysis and neurobiology at hand? Journal of the American Psychoanalytic Association, 45 (3), 807-840.

Sedgwick, D. (2000). Answers to nine questions about Jungian psychology. Psychoanalytic Dialogues, 10 (3), 457-472.

Segal, H. (1983). The Function of Dreams. In M. Lansky, (Ed.), Essential papers on dreams. Lansky, M., Ed. (1992) New York: New York University Press.

Shengold, L. (1976). Book review: The Freud Jung letters. Journal of the American Psychoanalytic Association, 24 (3), 669-683.

Silberer (1909) Bericht uber eine methode, gerwisse symbolische. In The interpretation of dreams. Standard Edition IV and V. London: Hogarth Press.

Stern, D. (1985). The interpersonal world of the infant. New York: Basic Books.

Stekel, W. (1938). Technique of analytical psychotherapy. New York: Norton & Company.

Sullivan H. S. (1938). Introduction to the study of interpersonal relations. Psychiatry, 1, 121-134.

Sullivan H. S. (1940). Conceptions of modern psychiatry. New York: Norton.

Sutherland, J. (1993). The autonomous self. Bulletin of the Menninger Clinic, 57 (1), 3-32.

Ticho, E. (1980). The alternate schools and the self. Journal of the American Psychoanalytic Association, 30, 849-862.

Tronick, (1989) Emotions and emotional communication in infants. American psychologist, 44 (2), 112-119.

Tronick E. Z. (1998). Dyadically expanded states of consciousness and the process of therapeutic change. Infant Mental Health Journal, 19 (3), 290-299.

Tuttman, S. (1988). Psychoanalytic concepts of "the self." Journal of the American Academy of Psychoanalysis, 16 (2), 209-219.

Ulanov, A. (1999). Religion and the spiritual in Carl Jung. New York: Paulist Press.

Wallace, M. (1995). Introduction to Ricoeur's Freud & philosophy. New Haven, CT: Yale University Press.

Weiss, J. (1986, 1992). Dreams and Their Various Purposes. In M. Lansky, (Ed.), Essential Papers on Dreams. (1992) New York: New York University Press.

Whitmont, E. (1969). The Symbolic Quest. New York: Harper Colophon Books.

Winnicott (1970, 1989). On the basis of the self in body. In Winnicott, C.; Shepard, R.; Davis, M. (Eds.), Psychoanalytic explorations. (1989). Cambridge, MA: Harvard University Press.

Winnicott, D.W. (1949,1990). Mind and its Relation to the Psyche-Soma. In Through pediatrics to psychoanalysis. (1990). New York: Basic Books.

Winnicott, DW (1953, 1989). Review of psychoanalytic studies of the personality. In Winnicott, C.; Shepard, R.; Davis, M. (Eds.), Psychoanalytic explorations. (1989). Cambridge, MA: Harvard University Press.

Winnicott, DW (1960, 1965). The Theory of the Parent-Infant Relationship. In Maturational processes and the facilitating environment. (1965). London: Hogarth Press.

Winnicott, D.W. (1960a, 1965). Ego Distortion in Terms of True and False Self. In Maturational processes and the facilitating environment. (1965). London: Hogarth Press.

Winnicott, DW (1962, 1965). Ego Integration in Child Development. In Maturational processes and the facilitating environment. (1965). London: Hogarth Press.

Winnicott, DW (1963, 1965). From Dependence towards Independence. In Maturational processes and the facilitating environment. (1965) London: Hogarth Press.

Winnicott, DW (1963a, 1965). Morals and Education. In Maturational processes and the facilitating environment. (1965). London: Hogarth Press.

Winnicott, D.W. (1964). Book review: Memories, dreams, reflections. International Journal of Psycho-analysis, 45, 450-455.

Winnicott, DW (1968, 1989). Use of an Object and Relating Through Identifications. In Winnicott, C.; Shepard, R.; Davis, M. (Eds.)., Psychoanalytic explorations. (1989). Cambridge, MA: Harvard University Press.

Winnicott, DW (1971). Playing and reality. New York: Basic Books.

Waldhorn, H. (1967). Implications for Psychoanalysis: The Place of the Dream in Clinical Psychoanalysis. In Joseph, E. (Ed.)., (Monograph II of the Kris Study Group of the New York Psychoanalytic Institute). New York: International University Press.

Wolstein, B. (1975). Toward a conception of unique individuality. Contemporary Psychoanalysis, 11 (2), 146-160.

Zabriskie, B. (2000). The psyche as a process. Psychoanalytic Dialogues, 10 3, 389-402.

Zane, M. (1971). Significance of differing responses among psychoanalysts to the same dream. In J. Masserman, (Ed.), <u>Science and psychoanalysis,</u> volume 17. New York: Grune and Stratton.

www.ingramcontent.com/pod-product-compliance
Lightning Source LLC
Chambersburg PA
CBHW060626290526
45793CB00001B/155